RUN FOR GOD

The 5K Challenge
Fourth Edition

A practical guide to running and a 12-week training plan with a Christ centered focus.

Mitchell Hollis

Disclosures

Unless otherwise indicated, all Scripture taken from the New King James Version®. Copyright © 1982 by Thomas Nelson, Inc. Used by permission. All rights reserved.

Copyright © 2020 Run for God, LLC. All rights reserved.

All rights reserved. No part of this book may be reproduced, stored in a retrieval system, or transmitted in any other form or by any means without the prior written permission of the author.

ISBN: 978-1-7338732-1-5

Printed in the United States of America.

If you require medical, fitness, or nutritional advice, you must contact your own health care professional. You should seek the advice of a doctor before starting any exercise routine.

This book may contain information relating to various medical conditions and their treatment and an exercise/nutrition protocol. Such information is provided for informational purposes only and is not meant to be a substitute for the advice of a physician or health care professional. You should not use this information for diagnosing or treating a health problem or injury.

To make informed health care decisions, you should always consult your physician for your personal medical needs. Neither Run for God nor its agents, affiliates, partners, or licensors are providing these materials to you for the purpose of giving you medical advice.

For any questions about your health and well-being, please consult your physician.

Attention

Please be aware that all Run for God material is copyrighted and the Run for God logo is a registered trademark of the Run for God Organization.

No copies shall be made of this book, nor shall the logo be copied or used in any way without prior written consent of Run for God, Inc.

For questions regarding our copyright or trademark policy please contact CustomerService@RunforGod.com.

Thank you for your understanding.

The Run for God Team

No Copying Book

Table of Contents

Disclosures	ii
Meet the Authors	vi
Getting Started	viii
Week 1 : Introduction	3
Week 2 : Shoes and Fellowship	19
Week 3 : Gear and Run Your Race	39
Week 4 : Injuries and The Long Haul	59
Week 5 : Streching / Core and Hurry	77
Week 6 : Weight Loss and The Turning Point	95
Week 7 : Motivation and Jesus Wept	111
Week 8 : 5 Minute Mile and Concerto #55	129
Week 9 : What is Run for God?	145
Week 10 : Moving Past the Question	159
Week 11 : Running with God and Lifestyle	177
Week 12 : Silent Running with God and Race Day	189

If at anytime during this journey you would like to learn how to have Peace with God, please visit www.RunforGod.com/PeaceWithGod to learn how to do just that.

Enjoy the journey!

Meet the Authors

You may notice pretty quickly that there are two different writing styles contained in this manual. You're not reading the words of a person with multiple personalities, but you are reading the words of two separate people. This was done completely on purpose and for an excellent reason. It is our hope that our approach has led us to a more thorough and well-thought plan than one person would accomplish.

First, please understand that neither of us is a professional writer, but we do have two things in common: a love for Christ, our savior, and a love of running. You won't find the eloquence of Shakespeare, or the knowledge of Einstein, but you will find heartfelt thoughts and feelings that are our attempt to build you up both physically and spiritually.

Mitchell Hollis' focus was to look at the writing of the book from the instructor's point of view. The Instructor has a big job coordinating a Run for God class, and Mitchell's goal was to provide all the tools, reminders,

Meet the Authors

scripture support, and spiritual material needed to ensure the Instructor has all he/she needs to run (pun intended) a successful and impactful class. As the founder and instructor of the first Run for God class in the history of the Earth, there could be no one with more, or better, experience.

Dean Thompson's focus was to look at the writing of the book from the student's point of view. He provided the educational material and focused on ensuring that the student would be able to receive the most beneficial information we could provide. He is a lifetime runner, Run for God instructor, and has forgotten more running experiences than he remembers. Part of that could be due to his age! As a proficient runner, his perspective speaks from tens of thousands of road miles.

Introduction

Week 1

Take Personal Inventory

What are my goals for this week?

to complete Run for God week 1 training

What are the things that I need to pray for this week?

What are the challenges that potentially lay ahead this week?

weather, proper clothing & overcome sleep.

Why are you here?
Think long and hard about this question. Why did you decide to take part in the Run for God - 5K Challenge?

I want to run again but with a purpose. I want to get in shape. I want to run a marathon, not just dream about it would

Week 1 : Introduction

Why are you here at a Run for God class?

Before getting started, I would like you to think for a few minutes about this question. Write your answer on the previous page or the blanks below.

_____

_____

_____

The answer that I have heard more than any is, "I need to get in shape." Although there is no right or wrong answer, it is a good idea to put your answer in writing so that you can refer to it from time to time, because it may change. You may have written "I need to get into shape," or "I want to be around for my kids," or "I want to grow closer to God." You may even have said all of the above.

Whatever your reason, it is my hope and prayer that you will enjoy the sport of running and at the same time strengthen or even find your faith in the maker of all things, Jesus Christ.

Why did I, Mitchell want to write a Christian Running Devotional?

You know, I don't know if I have fully gotten an answer to that question just yet. With that said, I do feel that I know what led me to where I am today.

I started running in January 2007, and I was hooked from the moment I started. A few friends of mine were signing up for the Peachtree Road Race set for July 4, 2007, in Atlanta, Georgia. We all signed up and trained like a bunch of guys who thought we knew everything about the sport. We didn't have a plan, we didn't ask for advice, and we didn't think we needed any. We just knew that we had to cover 6.2 miles in the dead of summer, and it didn't matter how we did it as long as we finished. Well, finish is about all we did. Most of the Kenyans (the fast guys) were already

Week 1 : Introduction

on a plane back to their home country by the time we crossed the finish line. Some of us were sore, some of us were so burned out we would never run again, and some of us had just caught a glimpse of something that we knew we could not get enough of.

One of the guys who caught a glimpse was me. I came home complaining of hurting in places I had never hurt before and began trying to convince my wife Holly that we needed to do a marathon. At first, she told me that I was off my rocker and that there was no way she could do a marathon. I finally convinced her that there was no way I could do a marathon right now either but that in just six short months we could. The fact that we would be doing the Disney Marathon also helped a little.

So Disney it was. We signed up and started this adventure together, for better or worse. The next six months were tough. We would train together and separate. She would watch the kids (who were two and six at the time) while I ran, and then I would watch the kids while she ran. Just a few months before, we would get a sitter so we could enjoy dinner and a movie; whereas, now, we were getting a sitter to go run. If it was a really special occasion, we would get a sitter, run the Chattanooga River Walk, go change and wipe off with a washrag in the local public restroom, and have some pizza downtown. Needless to say, we were committed!

It didn't seem very long until it was time for Disney—Disney was here, ready or not. We felt good about our training and felt that we had done all we could do in such a short period of time. The only problem was that I had a stomach bug and really didn't know if I would finish that thing or not. With that said, almost six hours and what felt like ten restrooms later, we crossed the finish line. That night, every muscle in every part of our bodies hurt, but it was great! At least for me it was. Holly calls me a bit of a pain junkie. We felt like we had accomplished something, even if we did have to walk downstairs sideways to stop the sharp pains from shooting up our legs.

This experience only fueled my fire even more. I was already starting to think of what I could do next. I knew I had to improve my marathon time. What about ultra- marathons? And how about triathlons? Those looked fun, too. I was like a kid who had just learned that you really wouldn't drown if you jump off the diving board. I wanted to do more… a lot more.

In 2008 and 2009 I completed one 5K, five 10Ks, four 10 milers, three half marathons, two marathons, one 208-mile relay, one bike race, four triathlons, and one half Ironman. I got to where I loved endurance sports. It seemed like it was all I wanted to do or even talk about. Holly has supported me 100 percent and I cannot thank her enough for that. We even got our son Lane involved in Iron Kids, where he did great, even placing seventh at the national finals in Tucson, Arizona.

Through all that, I remained what I thought was faithful. I tried to be at church every time the doors were open, and I often thought about how I could start a running ministry. I came up with the logo on the cover of this book almost two years before it was written, and I even had breakfast with my pastor from time to time, but I was often convicted of not spending enough time with God and in his word. I knew what God was saying, but I just didn't have enough time for him. I could spend fifteen to twenty hours a week in the final months before an Ironman event biking, running, swimming, and cramming my head full of secular music through my MP3 player, but I couldn't find fifteen to twenty minutes a week to be alone with God.

Well, I am convinced that God will do anything he wants to get your attention, even if it means getting your attention at times you least expect it. You see, in October 2009 I had just finished my first half Ironman and had just gotten back from Lane's Iron-Kids event in Tucson. Needless to say I had plenty to talk about. At our church's homecoming lunch I sat down beside some friends of mine, H.R. and Adrian Poe. I have known H.R. and Adrian for most of my life. They have always been solid, mature Christian leaders in my eyes, and they both also love to run. It seems like every time I get a chance to speak to them that is where the conversation ends up and this day was no different. H.R. and I were talking running, triathlons, Lane's race, and how I had committed to the Florida Ironman in 2010. After we had talked for a few minutes, H.R. looked at me, his face as serious and concerned as it could be, and said, "Mitch, don't let this become your God." Wow, I thought, where in the world did that come? Here I am talking about running, traveling, and my kids, and H.R. is trying to give me pointers on my faith.

It wasn't until that night that H.R.'s words really began to sink in. I started thinking back on the past few years at all the hints God had given me, like the idea of this running ministry that I had just dismissed. God had put someone, someone in my running world, in my path to get my attention and set me straight. Over the next few days, I could not stop thinking about what H.R. had said and how he said it. Within a day or two I had dragged out the logo that I had sketched a few years ago. I knew I had to do one of two things: either stop using this sport that I love as an idol and an excuse, or use it to further God's kingdom.

Very likely, you are unable to tell by reading this book that I am not very comfortable sharing what God is doing in my life. This is where the logo comes in. One Saturday afternoon, a few weeks after that conversation with H.R., I showed up on his doorstep with some T-shirts that had this funny-looking stick man on them. They read, "Run for God."

I remember when some friends of mine and I did the Blue Ridge Relay in 2008. We had team shirts made that said, "Running for Katie." Below that they said, "My cup runneth over." Katie was a young lady in our community who had died from acute myeloid leukemia. In the final months before her death she questioned why she was sick, she missed her daughter Merriwether during the months she spent in the hospital, she cried when the doctors told her the leukemia had returned, but she never rejected her faith in God's love for her. In her final letter to her friends and family, she implored them to tell someone about Jesus. I remember being amazed at how many people came up to us and asked about our shirts and the story behind them. I told H.R. and Adrian that story, and how it was the reason behind my stick-man shirts. I told them that from now on I would be sporting one of these shirts while running, whether on the treadmill at the local gym or in my next marathon. Maybe this would force me to get out of my comfort zone and share what God was doing in my life, because I knew people were going to ask about my funny-looking shirt.

Even with all this, I still felt that I needed to do more. I tried to figure out how I could get others to wear the shirts. Then I thought, what better people to sport these fashionably correct shirts than people who love to run and love the Lord? This also got me thinking about the people over the years who have told me that they would like to get into running, but just didn't know where to start. That is where this book was born. I hope I can teach you a little about running and that we can teach each other a lot about our enduring faith, all the while telling others about the great God we serve.

Mission Statement

Preparing people to be better witnesses for Christ Physically, Mentally, and Spiritually

Physically—Create a healthier you and make it possible to reach a new demographic of non-believers—potential believers!

Go therefore and make disciples of all the nations, baptizing them in the name of the Father and of the Son and of the Holy Spirit, teaching them to observe all things that I have commanded you; and lo, I am with you always, even to the end of the age. Amen. Matthew 28:19–20

Mentally—Learn the discipline and endurance that it takes to "Run the Race Set Before Us."

Therefore we also, since we are surrounded by so great a cloud of witnesses, let us lay aside every weight, and the sin which so easily ensnares us, and let us run with endurance the race that is set before us. Hebrews 12:1

Spiritually—Learn always to give God the glory for all that we accomplish.

I will praise You, O Lord my God, with all my heart, And I will glorify Your name forevermore. Psalms 86:12

Objectives

To introduce the sport of running and to help you learn all that you need to know in order to make it enjoyable, satisfying, and rewarding.

To understand the pitfalls that can come from letting anything become an idol to you.

To understand the parallels of enduring a sport like running with enduring faith.

To understand how to become a better witness while doing something that you enjoy.

What are some things that typically become "idols" in your life?

Sleep, TV

What are some similarities between running and faith?

Must be committed, stand strong no matter what, keep going, consistent.

Disclosures

What qualifies me, Mitchell, to write this book?

I have never been asked this question before but I know people have thought it, so I thought it better to answer this question right up front. The answer is nothing other than my God wanting me to do more. You see, there is nothing groundbreaking or earth shattering about this book. I have simply taken what I feel the Lord has shown me and reduced it to writing. You can agree with me or you can disagree with me, but whatever you do, pray about it and agree with what God is telling your heart!

Run for God Format

Accountability Meetings. Your group should hold meetings once a week. You can meet at your church, at a gym, or at someone's home, depending on your group size. These meetings should consist of reviewing and discussing the weekly Bible study as well as new topics on running.

Training Days. Plan to train three days a week, preferably skipping a day between each workout: Tuesday, Thursday, Saturday or Monday, Wednesday, Saturday. It is a good idea to plan these workouts ahead just as if they were meetings or ball games. It is much easier to plan ahead than just "trying to fit it in."

Race Day! Count ahead twelve to fourteen weeks and book the date! Find a 5K that your group would like to attempt, and commit to it. Call the race director and discuss your plans. Ask if your group would be welcome, tents, screaming supporters, and all. I am sure the race organizers will support you 100 percent. Once booked, tell your friends, family, and church what you have done and why you have done it. Use this conversation to start your witness and your "Run for God" ministry.

Some Topics We Will Cover

While we will not be able to cover everything there is to know about running, we will be able to hit the most important topics of the sport. Below are just a few of these topics.

Shoes	Injuries	Core Exercises
Stretching	Nutrition	Cross Training
Goals	Recovery	Gear
Hydration	Race Day Preparation	Sore vs. Hurting

[Handwritten note: ★ Don't go on a diet @ this time]

Week 1 : Introduction

Running 101. Races?

All too often, I find myself speaking to someone about this race or that race and they begin asking, "Now, how far is that?" Below are the most common race distances in the sport of running.

1 Mile Fun Run — 1 mile
5K — 3.1 miles (The most popular beginner race)
10K — 6.2 miles
10 Miler — 10 miles
Half Marathon — 13.1 miles (The stepping stone to a marathon)
Marathon — 26.2 miles (The goal of most serious runners)
Ultra-Marathon — Anything over 26.2 miles

Need to Know NOW!

Many of the items below will be covered much more in the following chapters, but we thought it would be a good idea to briefly discuss a few of them now.

1. Set a Goal. This is a must! Sign up for a race and commit. Tell your friends, family, and others what you have done and let them help hold you accountable.

2. Start Slowly. Do not try to do too much, too fast. Listen to your body, follow your routine, and do not skip ahead! This only leads to burnout and possible injury.

3. Shoes, Shoes, Shoes. Do not go out this week and buy new running shoes. Running shoes are very unique to your foot type and should NOT be chosen by color and style. We will be covering shoes in detail next week, so please be patient!

4. Warm Up and Cool Down. Warming up your legs gets the blood flowing where it needs to in order to avoid injury, and cooling down helps your body flush out toxins like lactic acid that prohibit speedy recovery.

5. Rest, Rest, Rest. Many people think that muscle is built while working out. In reality, the opposite is true. Muscle fiber is torn and damaged during your workout, while rest allows that tissue to repair itself and become more efficient. So, while you want to have quality workouts, you must have equal quality in your rest periods.

6. Hydration is Key. Keep your body hydrated, even when you are not exercising. Take a water bottle to work or school. Staying regularly hydrated will benefit you when it comes time to run.

7. Think of Food as Fuel. Now is not the time for a crash diet. While you may lose weight during this process, it's not the focus. We will address nutrition in more detail later on, but for now keep a good balance of carbs and protein in your diet and just eat sensibly!

8. Get the Family Involved. Nothing will make this journey easier than having the support of your family and friends. One way or another, get them involved!

Where and When Should You Run?

Remember that a workout can fit into many aspects of your day, but the most important thing is to schedule it just like you do everything else.

Where	When
In your neighborhood	Early, before the day starts
Secondary roads	Lunch break
Parks	Afternoon, before dinner
Tracks (middle and high schools)	While the kids are at ball practice
Sidewalks	On your way home from work
Treadmill	Make a day of it: take the kids and bikes

Other Local Locations

_____

_____

Week 1 : Introduction

Remember to keep the following things in mind:

If you feel sore, keep going. If you feel pain, stop! We are starting with jogging, not running. Keep a slow pace and let your body adjust to the new sensations over the next few weeks. This may feel easy for some, but whatever you do, do not skip ahead. This is very tempting, but it can only lead to injuries and frustration.

Conclusion

I want to thank you for taking this journey with me. It is my hope and prayer that you will find the true joy that comes with this great sport that I love, a joy that can only be magnified if you do it to glorify our great and awesome God. Remember to keep your priorities in check and use others to help keep you accountable.

Weekly Notes

- Made all 3 days
- Run outside over 21°
- Check on socks for feet

Workout Journal

Week 1

Workout #1
Start with a brisk 5-minute warm-up walk. Then alternate 60 seconds of jogging and 90 seconds of walking for 20 minutes. Follow that with a 5-minute cool-down walk.

Total Workout = 30 Minutes

Workout #2
Start with a brisk 5-minute warm-up walk. Then alternate 60 seconds of jogging and 90 seconds of walking for 20 minutes. Follow that with a 5-minute cool-down walk.

Total Workout = 30 Minutes

Workout #3
Start with a brisk 5-minute warm-up walk. Then alternate 60 seconds of jogging and 90 seconds of walking for 20 minutes. Follow that with a 5-minute cool-down walk.

Total Workout = 30 Minutes

Be sure to download The 5K Challenge App which can be found in your app store.

Tues

Workout #1

Date _____Distance _____Time _____

Notes _____

_____

Weather   _____

Thurs

Workout #2

Date _____Distance _____Time _____

Notes _____

_____

Weather   _____

Sat

Workout #3

Date _____Distance _____Time _____

Notes _____

_____

Weather   _____

Running Shoes

Week 2

Take Personal Inventory

What are my goals for this week?
Continue & complete Tue/Thurs & Sat
workout.

What are the things that I need to pray for this week?

What are the challenges that potentially lay ahead this week?
Weather.

> Reflect back on the past week and take inventory. What went right? What went wrong? What were some of the highlights? Be specific.

- Did not want to get up
- But remained focus & made self go Run

Week 2 : Shoes and Fellowship

Main Story : Just Here for the Fellowship

My name is Tammy Ellison, I was approached by Mitchell Hollis in the hall at Grove Level Baptist Church in December of 2009. He told me he was starting a class that would teach me how to run, and we would complete the class with a 5k at the end. It would be the first ever Run for God class. We would also be doing a Bible study, which is what attracted me. I wasn't really interested in the running part because I have never been a runner. I did like the idea of the Bible study and fellowship time. So, I went to the first class.

Please understand, Run for God was not even a "thing" yet. We didn't have books, videos, or anything official at that point. He asked us why we were there and most everyone said, "To get in shape and get in the Bible more." He read from the notes he had written on a sheet of paper telling us a little about the Bible verses he asked us to read from our Bibles, and told a little bit about running and what we would be doing for the next 12 weeks.

The next week it was time to run. Again, he read our devotion from a piece of paper, and we read verses from our Bible he had selected to go along with the discussion. I still had no desire to run, but I liked spending time with my Fellow Christ Believers, so I kept going. I remember starting with 5 minutes of walking to warm up. Then he told us to run. It lasted 60 seconds, but it felt like 60 minutes!

Some of us decided to meet up during the week for the other workouts. It was so hard, but having my new friends along certainly helped. We were all going through the same tough battle. Isn't that the best part of being with our Christian friends? The support is amazing.

We moved to 90 seconds of running, then 3 minutes, and 5 minutes, until we reached the 8th week when we would have to run for 20 minutes. Yes! I did it! Every step of the way!

During this 12-week study/run class I grew closer to the Lord. As I walked/jogged/ran outside, I enjoyed God's beautiful creation. I listened to the birds chirping and sometimes saw deer running when I ran through the Chickamauga Battlefield. It was a time I could be alone with God and His beautiful creation. I often had my running buddies Gaye and Kim to talk to as well. We would complain, whine, and laugh about why we were running but we enjoyed each other's company - so we continued. We were amazed at the progress we made from the first 60 second run.

The day finally came when it was time to run my first ever race. It was a 5k and I was a nervous wreck. But I made it. I finished my race physically, but I am still running the spiritual race of life. I press on toward the goal to win the prize for which God has called me heavenward in Christ Jesus.

Tammy Ellison – Ringgold, GA

Get in the Word

But those who wait on the Lord Shall renew their strength;
They shall mount up with wings like eagles, They shall
run and not be weary, They shall walk and not faint.
Isiah 40:31

I can do all things through Christ who strengthens me.
Philippians 4:13

Nevertheless you have done well that you shared in my distress.
Philippians 3:14

Something to Ponder

Who first encouraged you to start running?
My friend Pamela.

Who is your support team?
My family

Do you have a church family to turn to in the times you struggle?

Yes (handwritten)

Education : Introduction to Running Shoes

If you have ever been to a shoe store and gazed at the hundreds of footwear choices, you know that choosing a running shoe is a daunting task! The good news is that some education about how they work can make choosing a shoe that is right much easier. What you will find out is although there are hundreds of shoes to choose from, there are only a few that are right for you. Choosing the proper running shoe is not about style or color as much as it is about fit, feel and performance.

Your choice of footwear may be the most important decision you make as a runner. It is your foundation. We all know the parable of the man who built his house on sand and how destructive that decision was for him. We also know, from the same parable that the man who built his house on firm ground turned out to be the wiser. Think of your footwear the same way. If you wear improper shoes, it will not be as fun, will hurt more than it should, and it's very likely you'll end up injured.

When you run, you are producing an impact on your body equal to three to five times your body weight. Think about that number for a few seconds, and then multiply that number times the number of steps you take while running. Minimalizing that impact is critical to your running success.

$$150 \text{ lbs.} \times 4 = 600 \text{ lbs.}$$
$$\text{STEP} = 600 \text{ lbs.}$$
$$\text{STEP} \times 5{,}000 \text{ STEPS}$$

MILE = 3,000,000 lbs.

Shoes are technical, so as much as we will try to help you understand all about running shoes, nothing can replace the expertise of someone who works in a specialty running store. If it is possible for you to get to one of these establishments, it is the best thing you can do, especially when purchasing your first pair of running shoes. The people who work there have an interest in ensuring that you continue to run for a long time. They want to build relationships with you.

Be selfish in your running shoe choice. Find the right shoe regardless of price. You will be happy later! Just one word of caution, don't buy a shoe just because someone else tells you it is a good shoe. While it may be a great shoe for them, it may not be what you need. After learning about how they work, you'll understand why. This choice is all about you, and you alone.

What do I need to consider before buying my shoes?

One thing you will learn about becoming a runner is that everyone will now expect you to be an expert on running shoes. People will ask you questions about running shoes, and you want to be able to give them the best answers possible. So, it is important, not only to you but for the benefit of others, for you to know what to consider as you walk into the store to purchase your running shoes.

Pronation

Most people have heard this word, but have a difficult time explaining it. Some people even think that pronation is a bad thing that they need to hide. Explaining to the sales associate that they think they have a "pronation thing" can be difficult. And, they're right! We all do! Pronation is simply the way a foot moves through the step cycle from the time the foot hits the ground until it is up on the toes. There are different things that happen when you pronate and that is where the key lies. Knowing what your particular foot does during each step is most important in determining what shoe to purchase. The best way to know your pronation tendencies is to either video your foot-strike from behind while running on a treadmill, or have someone run behind you and watch what your foot does as your roll through your steps. Say it loud: "I'm a pronator and proud of it!"

Foot shape

All feet are different shapes and sizes. Are your feet wide or narrow? Do you have a high arch or flat feet? Is your second toe your longest toe? Do you have bunions, or anything that makes your foot unique? Maybe you have duck feet, wide in the front and narrow in the heel. Knowing your foot shape will help determine what shoes will be most comfortable and effective for your feet.

Fit

A properly fitting shoe will be comfortable, both while you are sitting as well as when you are running. Your foot swells when you run, so it's important to ensure that your shoe is the proper size. You should have a thumbnail length from the end of your longest toe (not necessarily your big toe) to the end of the shoe. This is a big change for some folks as they begin to run. Someone who usually wears shoes that fit closer to the end of the foot will feel like the shoe is too large. And, some have a difficult time accepting the fact that, although they normally wear a size seven, they will need to wear an eight in running shoes. Resist the temptation to wear a shoe that is functionally too small. There is no place for vanity when choosing your running shoe size! The rest of the shoe should feel good with no slipping from the heel and no sloppiness in the forefoot. It should feel almost like part of your foot.

Feel

Your running shoes should feel good on your feet, but it is important to realize that everyone has different preferences. Some like a shoe that is very soft, while others like a firmer feel. To some, a light shoe feels great. Some shoes are designed to have a more severe or less severe drop from front to back and this will affect the feel quite a lot. The important thing to remember is that feel is subjective. While you can have an ill-fitting shoe, the determination of whether or not a shoe feels good is entirely up to the wearer. Don't stop with the first shoe that feels good, you may find one that feels better!

Ride

Have you ever worn shoes that feel like you have to work harder to walk in them than it does to just walk barefoot? That is a poor ride. You want your shoes to feel like they complement the way you walk or run. It should feel like they are part of your feet, helping you to get through each step. They should aid your biomechanics, not work against them.

Midsole

There are two things to consider about the midsole of any running shoe and how it fits you, individually. Of course, we always think about the cushioning in the midsole and that is an important factor in choosing the running shoe that is best for you. Understanding the amount of cushioning you prefer is part of the "feel" and the "ride" of the shoe that we covered. The second factor to consider is how the shoe works with your particular pronation tendencies. Finding the shoe that works best for your biomechanics is critical to feeling good when you run and preventing injuries. There are three general categories of pronation, though there are varying degrees of each.

Over-pronation

Right Foot Over Pronation

Over-pronation happens when a foot rolls further towards the arch side of your foot than is normal. Nearly everyone's foot rolls inward as they step, so the motion is normal, but over-pronators' feet just roll a little further. This causes stress on the lower body and can lead to injuries if not corrected. The foot should remain balanced as it begins to roll up onto the ball of your foot. Running shoe manufacturers have figured out how to build shoes that accomplish the task of keeping you balanced.

When you look at a running shoe, you will find, on the arch side of the shoe, that there are often two different colors of midsole. Upon further inspection, you will find that one of the colors is softer than the other. The firmer material is placed under the inside of the foot to aid in keeping the foot from rolling too far inward. For an over- pronator, this type of shoe is critical. However, it is also important to remember that not all over-pronators are created equally. The varying degrees are infinite, but the running shoe companies have created shoes for that diversity. Now, it is beginning to make sense why there are so many shoes on that wall! If you pick up two shoes made by the same manufacturer, you can tell which one is made for the more severe over- pronator because the componentry will be more substantial.

Remember that the focus should be on keeping the foot balanced as it rolls forward. For this reason, it is important to buy the shoe that is made for your particular biomechanics. You can see why it is so important to be evaluated individually.

Neutral Pronation

A second category of pronation focuses on the person whose foot rolls inward a little, but not excessively. This motion is natural and serves as the body's shock absorber as you run. In the analysis of pronation, it is important to know where the line is between neutral and over-pronation. The neutral pronation runner does not need any correction, so the shoe should not have any of the componentry that exists to prevent over-pronation. These shoes are usually identified with mid-soles and lack the two- color concept the over-pronator shoes contain.

Neutral

Although a neutral runner could wear a shoe with very mild correction properties, there is no need for it. The extra features make the shoe more expensive and there is no need to pay for something you don't need. In the worst case, a shoe made for more severe over-pronators could push the neutral runner over the outside of the heel and cause stress on the outer part of the leg which will eventually lead to injury. Remember that the key to keeping the trauma to your legs to a minimum is both cushion and balance. Keeping the foot as balanced as possible as it rolls through the pronation process is important.

Under-Pronation (Supination)

The final category is reserved for those who under pronate, also known as supination. The truth is that this segment of the population is very small. Chances are slim that you are a supinator, but if you are one of the few, you will need a shoe with no componentry on the medial or inside of your shoe. Any correction at all will only serve to make the problem worse. Before you declare that you think you are an under-pronator, please see the section on running shoe myths.

Right Foot Supination

Cushioning

When you look at the shoes on someone's feet and notice that they are running shoes, what distinguishes them from other shoes? For the most part, the thicker, flared heel gives it away. That's where the cushioning lives. There was a time when there were not many choices in running shoes and you had to choose between a highly structured shoe and a soft, cushioned shoe. Today, there are structured shoes that are cushioned, as well.

The cushioning choices are almost endless as there are shoes all along the spectrum from soft to firm. We all have different preferences for what feels best to us. In order to find what shoe is most comfortable for you, you will need to run in the shoes. Don't be afraid to run up and down the aisles to get a feel for your shoes. The right amount of cushioning is a personal preference, and only you can identify yours.

Shoes will last about 300 to 500 miles. That lifespan is based on the cushioning, not the outsole. After these miles, the cushioning can become inadequate and there will be additional stress on your lower body that you do not want. Remember that shoes wear out slowly, so you will not have a day when you realize the cushioning disappeared overnight. Also, realize that a shoe's lifespan is all about miles, not time. It is the number of times the shoe is compressed that determines when it is worn out.

Upper

The upper is the part of shoe that covers your foot. The important thing to remember about the upper is that it should be breathable. Make sure that there is an open mesh made from synthetic materials covering your foot. Any technically capable running shoe will have the proper materials in the upper, so as long as you are buying a high quality shoe, this will not be a factor for concern. It is a factor, however, if you are a walker. There is nothing wrong with being a walker and, if you are a walker, be proud of it! There are "walking" shoes on the market that are made of leathers and synthetic leathers that are simply not very breathable. Walkers should wear running shoes for breathability.

Outsole

The outsole is the part of shoe that comes in contact with the ground. You will typically notice that running shoes have a firmer substance on the outside of the heel and in the forefoot than the rest of the outsole. This substance is usually carbon rubber and is tougher than the rest of the outsole. Shoes are reinforced in the areas of most wear, and most runners land on the outside part of their heel and push off with the forefoot. The carbon rubber enables the outsole to last longer.

Running Shoes - Debunking the Myths

If you are to become the expert that people will now expect you to be, it is important that you know the common misconceptions about running shoes. You can play an integral part in preventing injuries and making others' running experiences more pleasant. There are four major myths to debunk.

Myth #1 - People believe they are under-pronators because of the wear pattern on their shoes.

Most people land on the outside part of their heel when they walk or run. This creates more friction; hence, more wear on the part of the shoe that strikes the ground first. All walkers and most runners will wear out the outside heel of their shoe first. A notable exception would be someone who lands on the midfoot or forefoot first. The truth is that the wear patterns on your shoes tell very little about your pronation tendencies and the wear pattern on the heel, specifically, tells you nothing. Many over-pronators will wear out the outside heel of the shoe first.

Myth #2 - Shoes are made for specific body sizes.

Let's look at two different runners. One is a six feet, three inch tall man who tips the scale at 240 pounds. The second is a petite, five feet, two-inch woman who weighs in at 105 pounds. Question: Could these two individuals be fitted properly for the same model shoe? Yes, they can. Why? Because they have the same pronation tendencies, the same foot shape, and have the same preferences for fit, feel and ride. Just because a shoe looks like it is more substantial and heavier does not mean it is made for a heavier body type. In the same way, a less substantial, lighter shoe is not necessarily made for a smaller, lighter runner.

Shoes are simply not made for a particular body type, but often, when someone begins to run, there is a substantial weight loss associated with the increased activity. Sometimes there is a tendency to believe that a different type of shoe is indicated for the change in body type, but it is not. It is okay, however, to celebrate that weight loss with a brand new, shiny pair of running shoes, because you earned it!

Myth #3 - A more expensive shoe means it is a better shoe.

You earn the money you spend and you want to spend it wisely. You can expect to pay between $80 and $150 for a good pair of technically capable running shoes.

You may see a pair at a local discount store for $40 and think you can save money by buying that shoe because it looks just like those $100 shoes at the running store, but don't be duped. The materials in that shoe are not the same as the technically capable shoe. Is it possible to find a shoe for less than $80? Sure, and here is an example of when it is okay to spend less. Running shoe companies often change models from year to year, and will consequently place the old model on sale. If it was good for you last year, it is certainly okay for you this year, too.

Some shoes have more bells and whistles than others. We have covered the need for more componentry in a shoe for an over-pronator and that will certainly lead to a higher price, but many features are non-essential. For example, a shoe may have a more plush material on the tongue to feel better against your skin if you wear low socks. Nice, sure. Necessary? Not for most. You can spend the extra money if you choose, just know the difference between what is necessary and what is non-essential.

Having said all that, don't be afraid to spend money. Find the shoe that is right for you and buy it. Once you spread the cost of a shoe over the multiple thousands of steps you will take in it, the differences are not that much. Buy the one that FEELS the best. Try to avoid buying the one that is most fashionable. Your feet will thank you for that.

Myth #4 - You can look at someone's arch and determine their pronation tendencies.

Many people will tell you that they have flat feet and, therefore they are over- pronators. While this may prove true many times, it is not true every time. Remember, pronation tendencies are determined by watching the foot as it pronates. You can tell very little about pronation tendencies by simply looking at the shape of a foot.

Our Enemy – Impact

There are two main functions of a running shoe. One is to keep your foot in alignment through the pronation cycle, and we have covered that. The second function is to protect you from the impact of running. As mentioned earlier, when you run, you are landing with the force of three to five times your body weight, so it is important to protect your body from the effects of that impact. What are the factors that determine the amount of impact you place on your body when you run?

Cushioning

The first factor is the amount of cushioning in your shoe, or more specifically, how much of the impact is absorbed into your shoe versus your body. Remember that the cushioning in your shoes will wear out over the miles and you should not use them for more than 500 miles. That will ensure that you always have adequate cushioning in your shoes. It is also very important to purchase a technically capable shoe. There are many injuries attributable to the use of inferior shoes.

Surface

The surface on which you choose to run plays a part in the amount of impact your body takes. Running on grass versus concrete will certainly lessen the impact to your body because the grass is softer than the concrete and will absorb some of the impact. Many treadmills provide impact-dampening protection, as well. It doesn't mean it is a bad idea to run on harder surfaces, but be aware of the effect it has on your body.

Biomechanics

There was a big push toward minimalism over the not too distant past that created shoes, which literally have no cushion to them at all. The premise behind those shoes is that the body is made to absorb shock, and that is absolutely true. However, most people have to change their biomechanics (running form) completely in order to run in these shoes. There are people who continue to run many miles in these types of shoes and that is because biomechanics are another factor in determining our impact. When someone looks lighter on his or her feet, it may very well be true! If you are a heel striker, or someone who lands on their heel first, you will have greater impact than someone who lands on their midfoot.

While the way you run determines impact, one way to lessen that impact is to run with a shorter stride. Keeping your feet below you instead of reaching out and landing with your foot ahead of you will minimize the impact on your body.

Weight

Last, but not least, is your weight. The heavier you are, the more impact you have to absorb. There is no way around this one, other than to lose weight, which may be why you are running to begin with! As you lose weight, you are lessening your potential for injury because it's easier on your body with every step. It's just one more reason to be excited about hitting that weight loss goal!

Conclusion

It is not hard to see why choosing the proper running shoe for you is important. If you have never been fitted for running shoes in the past, or have just begun running, do yourself a favor and make a trip to a running specialty store. They will take the time to fit you in a shoe that is right for you. Don't be afraid to take your time, try the shoes out and make sure you get the best bang for your buck. Cherish the relationships that you build with your local running store. They have a vested interest in your well-being.

I have taught you in the way of wisdom; I have led you in right paths. When you walk, your steps will not be hindered, And when you run, you will not stumble. Take firm hold of instruction, do not let go; Keep her, for she is your life. Proverbs 4:11-13

Quote of the Week

"Whether you think you can or you think you can't, you're right."
Henry Ford

Week 2 : Shoes and Fellowship

Notes

Workout Journal

Week 2

Workout #1
Start with a brisk 5-minute warm-up walk. Then alternate 90 seconds of jogging and 2-minutes of walking for 20 minutes. Follow that with a 5-minute cool-down walk.

Total Workout = 30 Minutes

Workout #2
Start with a brisk 5-minute warm-up walk. Then alternate 90 seconds of jogging and 2-minutes of walking for 20 minutes. Follow that with a 5-minute cool-down walk.

Total Workout = 30 Minutes

Workout #3
Start with a brisk 5-minute warm-up walk. Then alternate 90 seconds of jogging and 2-minutes of walking for 20 minutes. Follow that with a 5-minute cool-down walk.

Total Workout = 30 Minutes

Be sure to download The 5K Challenge App which can be found in your app store.

Workout #1

Date _____ Distance _____ Time _____

Notes _____

_____

Weather _____

Workout #2

Date _____ Distance _____ Time _____

Notes _____

_____

Weather _____

Workout #3

Date _____ Distance _____ Time _____

Notes _____

_____

Weather _____

Running Gear

Week 3

Take Personal Inventory

What are my goals for this week?
_____
_____
_____
_____

What are the things that I need to pray for this week?
_____
_____
_____
_____

What are the challenges that potentially lay ahead this week?
_____
_____
_____
_____

Reflect back on the past week and take inventory. What went right? What went wrong? What were some of the highlights? Be specific.

Week 3 : Gear and Run Your Race

Main Story : Run Your Race

Week three of the original Run for God class was probably the week that put everything in perspective for me. It's also from where our class theme, "Run Your Race" came. The lesson began with a story about Jimmy Page, the VP of Field Ministry for FCA (Fellowship of Christian Athletes). In the story, Jimmy tells about his first ever Triathlon and the advice he was given to "run his race" and not worry about the other competitors. Jimmy goes on to explain that he didn't heed the warning and in the first event he nearly drowned because he was trying to keep up with the more experienced and stronger racers. Jimmy finishes the story by saying, "I nearly had to quit… I got caught up in the excitement of the event and decided to abandon my plan and do what the other competitors were doing."

How many times do we do the same thing as Christians? So often we focus on works and what other people are doing. Perhaps we worry that we're not doing enough and start trying harder - only to feel like we are drowning. Before long, we find ourselves running a worldly race and trying to be good enough. Just like the Galatians, we find ourselves off course with no sight of our ultimate finish line (Galatians 5:7). The truth is we are eternally saved by grace; it is nothing we earned and nothing we do keeps it secured. God has designed your race, don't get off course, stick to His plan, and Run Your Race. Remember that once we determine to run our own race, there is still a race to be run. The race didn't end because we stopped following others. In fact, that is where the race gets hard!

As anyone who has completed the 5K Challenge can tell you, there is a lot of work that goes into preparing for a 5k. Hours are spent training, pain and injury are always a threat, and there are distractions and discouragements with each step. But with the finish line as our focus, we press on. Paul tells us in Hebrews 12:1 to, Lay aside every weight, and the sin which so easily ensnares us, and let us run with endurance the race that is set before us. We are to serve God, sharing the gospel with others. Paul knew his death was certain, but he ignored even that distraction so that he could serve God fully. Paul's ultimate goal was to be everything that Christ wanted him to be and he stayed focused and did not let anything hinder him – all the way to his finish line.

Much like a race, the Christian life is not easy. We have to invest our time, we face affliction, and feel pain. But with Christ as our ultimate goal we can ignore these distractions and keep going. At the finish line if you want to be able to say, I have fought the good fight, I have finished the race, I have kept the faith. 2 Timothy 4:7, then you will have to forget about all the distractions and Run Your Race.

Shawn McEver – Loganville, GA

Get in the Word

You ran well. Who hindered you from obeying the truth?
Galatians 5:7

Therefore we also, since we are surrounded by so great a cloud of witnesses, let us lay aside every weight, and the sin which so easily ensnares us, and let us run with endurance the race that is set before us,
Hebrews 12:1

I have fought the good fight, I have finished the race, I have kept the faith.
2 Timothy 4:7

Something to Ponder

How quickly do you find yourself following others and getting off course with your original goal out of focus?

___

What are those distractions that quickly get you off course?

___

How can you ensure that Christ is your ultimate focus and stay on course?

___

Education : Gear

We discussed the most important gear when we covered shoes in the previous chapter, but there are many other items, gadgets and garments to be aware of as a budding runner. Keep in mind that, although there are no substitutes for a pair of running shoes, most of the things we will cover in this chapter are optional. We will discuss the purpose behind each item and leave it up to you to determine whether it is worth spending your hard earned money on them. The good news is that many types running related clothing and gadgets are useful and/or stylish enough to use in other settings. That has not always been the case.

Clothing

After considering shoes, what you wear while you run will be the most important decision to make. There was a day when a runner would go down to the store and pick up a pair of gym shorts, a cotton t-shirt and maybe a sweatshirt and they were ready to go. That's probably where the idea of handing out t-shirts at races came from; it was one more training shirt. But those days are long gone. The choices are so much more comfortable and stylish these days. Of course, there are different seasons and climates to consider when choosing clothing. Another factor is personal choice, which we will cover as we go through the options.

Summer Clothing

For most climates, it is very warm in the summer, which often requires smart choices. When the temperature is 90 degrees, your clothing choices can provide some protection and help to keep you as cool as possible. Running will be much more difficult in the heat but can be done as long as you take precautions. The human body is meant to cool itself through sweating. As the moisture evaporates from your skin, it cools your body. Running apparel should work with your body's natural cooling system when running in the heat. Besides leaving your skin exposed in order to let the sweat evaporate, the materials used to make running apparel will help with moisture management. Today's running gear is made from synthetic materials that pull the moisture away from your skin and carry it to the surface of the garment to evaporate, which is an important feature, particularly in the summer.

Most runners wear shorts in the summer, allowing the skin on their legs to naturally cool themselves as they sweat. There are many choices for shorts, but running shorts should be made of a light, synthetic material to effectively keep you as cool as possible. Most are made with a liner that replaces your undergarments, which can become saturated with sweat and lead to chafing and cause raw places, most often, on the inside of the thighs where legs rub together. Other types of shorts can be worn, including shorts without liners, but it is important during the summer that they be made of a synthetic and light material.

Some prefer to wear short tights during the summer and that is okay. The shorter the tights are, the better. Tights are generally warmer than shorts, but they provide some support and compression that feels good to many runners. Wearing full tights or sweatpants during the summer is not recommended. There is a mindset that sweating more is good for you and will help you lose weight. The truth is that the weight loss is only temporary and the practice of running in sweats in the summer can be dangerous.

There are, seemingly, infinite choices for covering your upper body while running. T-shirts remain a popular way to cover up and keep cool during the summer. Just check the label on the shirt and make sure it is made from a synthetic material like polyester or nylon. Cotton shirts will soak up moisture as you sweat and hold it against your skin, which can become quite uncomfortable.

Sleeveless shirts and tank tops provide a runner with less coverage, which is more comfortable for most as it allows them to be cooler. They should still be made of the same materials as the t-shirts.

Another consideration is shirt color. Light colors are cooler than dark colors, which tend to soak up the sun's rays and make you warmer. Also, if you are going to be running where there is traffic, it is important to be easily seen. A runner is much easier to see when wearing a bright neon color as opposed to wearing gray. Running on a track or in a park makes the point moot. Again, there are many choices, but these general guidelines always apply.

Another suggestion during the summer would be headbands for keeping the sweat out of your eyes. There are a few advanced products on the market that help direct the sweat from your head away from your eyes. Cooling bandanas are another tool you can use to keep cool. They are soaked in water to keep cool water close to your skin when running. Hanging them around your neck keeps cooler water against your skin.

A final option, for men, is to run without a shirt, although it is not encouraged. It is certainly cooler, but it increases your exposure to the sun, which potentially has very bad consequences. Please see the section on sunscreen later in this chapter.

Winter Clothing

Keeping warm during winter runs is almost as important as keeping cool during the summer. Many runners will stop running during the winter because they don't like running in the cold weather. For some, it may be that they do not know how to dress in the winter. It is safe to run in the winter in most climates, as long as you take precautions. Running in the winter is even more individualized than running in the summer as runners have many preferences for comfort. The trick is to find the perfect place between being too cold from under-dressing and being too warm from over-dressing.

Many runners will continue to wear shorts in the winter down to temperatures in the twenties and even the teens. There is simply no standard for what temperature is appropriate to switch from shorts to leg coverage. It is all based on personal preference, and may even be determined by how far or how intense the run is going to be. Wind and cloud coverage is also a factor as wind chills and the bright shining sun can make the temperature feel colder or warmer than the actual temperature. Everyone has to find that line. Runners probably watch the weather as closely as anyone, timing their runs to capitalize on the best window of weather.

Do you wear pants or tights? Again, it is determined by personal preference, sometimes dictated by local tendencies. There are some parts of the country that have not embraced men wearing tights, and that's fine, because there are many choices for running pants. For women, tights have become as much a fashion statement as a running tool. Find your preference for temperature, material and type of leg covering through experimentation. If you find pants or tights too warm at fifty degrees, wear shorts and try tights at forty-five degrees. Just remember to wear synthetic materials. Know that there is no style standard, so if you are the only one in a group wearing long pants on a group run, that's okay. It's your preference, and there is, generally speaking, no right or wrong way to dress while running.

There are many choices of garments with long sleeves. We'll talk about each:

Long sleeve t-shirt - This is the lightest and least warm of the choices. Wear a long sleeve t-shirt when it is not super cold. You can wear a short sleeve t-shirt over or under a long sleeve shirt for a little more warmth.

Windbreakers - A windbreaker is a light jacket that is meant to provide protection from the wind. It is worn over a t-shirt or even a sweatshirt. Many times, a simple windbreaker over a t-shirt is just right on a not-too-cold, but windy day.

Sweatshirts/Hoodies - Any garment made from fleece provides a lot of warmth and is good for cold days. It is smart, however, to wear a shirt made of synthetic material under the fleece to help pull the moisture away from your skin as you sweat.

Jackets - There are many options in running jackets that span a large price range. Jackets are warmer than a windbreaker because they have a lining that adds another layer of warmth and protection. That lining can provide many different levels of warmth.

Rain Jackets - Although running in the rain may not be for everyone, rain jackets make it more comfortable. Make sure the jacket is breathable, though, as many raincoats are made from impermeable material that will not allow your moisture to escape making it very uncomfortable. They can be worn while it is snowing, as well, and will keep you nice and dry!

Running sleeves - These are sleeves that look like socks with the ends cut out of them! There are occasions when being able to pull your sleeves off during a run would be nice. These sleeves are often seen at cold races where they are worn in conjunction with a race tank top.

Gloves

Gloves are another cold weather necessity. Although you can wear any type of glove while running, there are gloves made particularly for running. Once again, they are made from synthetic materials for breathability and moisture management. Some are very light and provide just a little protection, while others have fleece linings to make them warmer. Still, other gloves have a shell around them to protect from the wind. Using light gloves is important because there are many times that you want to pull the gloves off after warming up. Some runners will use disposable gloves, knowing that they will be tossing them away after the first fifteen minutes of a run.

Headwear

There are several choices for headwear while running. If you are running in the frigid cold, you will want to keep your head and ears warm. You can wear a beanie, a knitted cap, a headband that covers your ears, earmuffs, or a baseball cap. Many people like to keep their head and ears warm and will choose an option that does both, a beanie or knitted cap. Others just like to keep their ears warm with a headband or earmuffs. Since your ears do not have significant blood flow, they tend to get very cold on frigid days.

Wearing a baseball cap provides a little warmth to the head, but not the ears. They may be appropriate for some winter running, but are very important for some in the summer to keep the sun off the head, particularly when susceptible to sun/skin issues, or in extreme sun intensity.

Compression Wear

There are many different types of compression wear available today. There are several reasons why runners wear compression gear, some cosmetic and some functional. It is available as full tights, shorts, thigh coverage or calf coverage, as well as upper body wear. Here are some reasons why runners wear compression gear:

Modesty - Some runners will wear compression shorts or short tights under shorts for less leg exposure.

Recovery - Compression gear increases the circulation of the area being compressed which speeds recovery as the muscles are able to repair themselves more quickly.

Muscle fatigue - Because of the increased blood flow, there is evidence to show that muscles fatigue more slowly when being compressed.

Moisture management - Compression gear is made of moisture- wicking synthetic materials.

Prevention of chafing and rashes - Since the garment is close to the skin, there is no rubbing of bare skin against other garments or body parts.

Undergarments - Some prefer to wear compression shorts under running shorts with no liner in place of underwear.

Socks

The socks you choose to wear while running can be nearly as important as the shoes you wear. A running sock made from moisture-wicking, synthetic material will keep your feet more dry and prevent blisters from forming. Sock preference varies quite a bit. That fact is noticeable when you see the many choices on the rack. Some are thick and some are thin. Some fit close while others are tight around your foot. Find what feels good to you, but make sure they fit snugly enough to prevent slippage and that they are made from the correct type of fabric.

Undergarments

Like socks, choice of underwear is important to your comfort while on the run. On the bottom, make sure there is no chance of chafing and holding moisture. As you run longer distances, this choice will become more and more important.

For ladies, your top is as individualized as fingerprints. There are many choices of sports bras on the market, so it makes choosing the perfect one a daunting task. Comfort is important, and there may not be a more important place to ensure materials are able to pull sweat away from your skin. You also want to reduce the amount of "bounce," and there are products designed with this issue specifically in mind. This is an area where it doesn't usually pay to be a cheapskate! Find quality materials made by a reputable company, and you will not regret it.

Layering

Any of the above choices can be combined in layers. Layering your clothing accomplishes two things: 1) It helps to join two different types of garments, like wearing a wind jacket over a hoodie on a cold and windy day. 2) It allows you to take off layers as you get too warm. For example, sometimes wearing a jacket and then taking it off and tying it around your waist after you warm up works very well.

A good rule of thumb is to dress for temperatures that are twenty degrees warmer than the actual air temperature.

Technology

Like every walk of life, there are new gadgets available to runners all the time. Most of them are luxury items that will not, in and of themselves, make you a better runner. Like a faster engine in a car, they may be nice to have, but they are not necessary. You can still get where you want to go with the basic engine.

Watches - The most basic of running technology is the watch, equipped with a timer so that you can see how long you have been running to monitor your pace. There are many more features to some watches as discussed below.

MP3 Players - Many runners like to listen to music, podcasts or books while they run. There are many choices for MP3 players and they are more affordable than ever. For many, running is an escape and listening to music or words furthers that experience. You can create playlists that are specific to running or songs that are inspirational to you to help you along the way. For your safety, always make sure that you play your music quiet enough to hear things going on around you. Also, never run with an MP3 player when you are on the road and there is traffic.

Heart-rate Monitors - These are devices that constantly monitor your heart rate, using a strap that goes around your chest. The chest strap will send the information to a wrist unit where you can see your heart rate in real time. Most have a connection to a computer where you can download the information and analyze it.

GPS - The availability to the general public of global positioning satellites has enabled us to use watches that know how far you have run, what pace you are running, the time since you began, and many other functions. Some are equipped with heart rate monitors, altitude and temperature measures, or even barometric readings! These devices are downloadable to your computer to enable you to analyze all of your runs in great detail.

Other Important Things

Sunscreen - If you are going to run under the sun, you should wear sunscreen. The link to skin cancer and sun exposure is well documented, so it makes sense to mitigate that exposure as much as possible. Always use sunscreen when running in the middle of the day when the sun is most potent. If possible, it is a good idea to run earlier or later in the summer months to avoid too much sun exposure. It is okay to run in the sun, just take precautions.

Sunglasses - When purchasing sunglasses, make sure they are going to feel good when you run, or have a special pair that you wear just for runs in the bright sun. It is no fun running in uncomfortable sunglasses.

Running at Night - When you run at night, it is important that you make yourself visible to others. Most running shoes have reflective areas on them, but there is clothing that has reflective logos and patches on them, as well. Going a bit farther, there are reflective vests available that provide both visibility and reflectivity. As previously mentioned, be sure to wear light colors too.

Water Bottle - Make it a habit to carry water with you any time you are going to run. Hydration is important, especially in the summer months. There are many types of water bottles. Find one you really like, and make it your constant companion.

Foam Rollers and Stick Rollers - Foam rollers are gaining popularity. They help you work out soreness and stiffness in your muscles by loosening and lengthening your muscles. Stick rollers are used for working out knots, or trigger points in muscles. These devices are not just for runners. They feel good for anyone with soreness, stiffness or trigger points. There are other massage tools that work your feet, your back, or anywhere else on your body. Check into them, they work!

Pain Relief - Most runners experience pain and/or soreness from time to time. The use of non-steroidal anti-inflammatories (NSAIDs) can be abused. Ibuprofen, for example, will alleviate pain or soreness, but be careful with it. Never take NSAIDs just before running because they can mask real problems. Remember, soreness is okay, pain is not. When you are sore, use it as a reminder of your accomplishments rather than masking it with drugs.

Publications - There is a plethora of information available today, both online and in print. Use the information as motivation! Find new ways to eat. Read stories about those who have overcome obstacles to become runners. There is no end to what you can find!

Need vs. Want

So, how much of this stuff do you really need? The truth is that, for most people, the only real requirement is a good pair of running shoes. That is one of the most wonderful things about running, everyone can do it! Don't get caught up in keeping up with the Joneses. If you can afford it, great, but don't feel pressured to have what others have. The running community, in general, is not a snooty bunch and will accept you, even encourage you, for whoever you are and whatever you wear!

The Most Important Gear

The most important tool in your bag is your Bible, for two reasons: 1) Encouragement is important and the Bible is full of verses to help motivate you to keep going. 2) You will meet many new people through running and many of them may not be Christians. You will need to equip yourself with the tools necessary to witness to others when they ask about your Run for God shirt. You may already be solid in this area, but sharpening your skills is always a good thing to do.

Paul explained it well in his second letter to Timothy:

All Scripture is given by inspiration of God, and is profitable for doctrine, for reproof, for correction, for instruction in righteousness, that the man of God may be complete, thoroughly equipped for every good work.
2 Timothy 3:16-17

Quote of the Week

"I never lost a game, I just ran out of time."
Vince Lombardi

Notes

_____

_____

_____

_____

_____

_____

Workout Journal

Week 3

Workout #1

Start with a brisk 5-minute warm-up walk. Then alternate 90 seconds of jogging and 2-minutes of walking for 20 minutes. Follow that with a 5-minute cool-down walk.

Total Workout = 30 Minutes

Workout #2

Start with a brisk 5-minute warm-up walk. Then alternate 90 seconds of jogging and 2-minutes of walking for 20 minutes. Follow that with a 5-minute cool-down walk.

Total Workout = 30 Minutes

Workout #3

Start with a brisk 5-minute warm-up walk. Then alternate 90 seconds of jogging and 2-minutes of walking for 20 minutes. Follow that with a 5-minute cool-down walk.

Total Workout = 30 Minutes

Be sure to download The 5K Challenge App which can be found in your app store.

Workout #1

Date _____ Distance _____ Time _____

Notes _____

_____

Weather _____

Workout #2

Date _____ Distance _____ Time _____

Notes _____

_____

Weather _____

Workout #3

Date _____ Distance _____ Time _____

Notes _____

_____

Weather _____

Injuries

Week 4

Take Personal Inventory

What are my goals for this week?
_____
_____
_____
_____

What are the things that I need to pray for this week?
_____
_____
_____
_____

What are the challenges that potentially lay ahead this week?
_____
_____
_____
_____

Reflect back on the past week and take inventory. What went right? What went wrong? What were some of the highlights? Be specific.

Week 4 : Injuries and The Long Haul

Main Story : In It for The Long Run

Have you ever felt when you are getting ready for a run that Satan grabs his shoes and heads out the door with you? His plan seems to be to stop you before you get started. He might start with a small thought like… "It might rain." "You don't really have time." "It's super-HOT." Or, "You are really tired." Then, seeing that those small thoughts didn't work, he throws sharper darts - "You should really just quit running altogether." "You will never win a medal." "You will never be as fast as someone else." Or, "You will never run a full marathon like other people your age."

He uses absolute negatives and really plays dirty. We need to knock him out with a 1-2 punch! PUNCH 1- I am convinced that Satan doesn't enjoy running with an unwavering, thankful heart. Begin each run by counting your blessings - "Thank you Lord for the health and ability to run." "Thank you for the gift of running and the restoration that it has brought to my life mentally, physically and spiritually." "Thank you for my family, friends and job." "Thank you for running with me today." By that time, you realize that Satan is no longer keeping up with you. He is falling way behind. Don't look back! Keep praying… "Lord, thank you for being the healing in my knee, the will in my heart, the breath in my lungs, the wind in my face, the push at my back and the truth in my head." You are the ultimate healer. You know my body, my strengths and limitations. You are the beauty in the nature and the restoration in the breeze. Let me hear your word instead of Satan's falsehoods. Let me hide your word in my heart." At this time, Satan is nowhere in sight, but just wait, he doesn't give up easily and will show back up when your body tires.

PUNCH 2- Remember the ultimate goal - Run with endurance. Hebrews 12:1. Well done good and faithful servant. Matthew 25:23. It's not just about this run or this day. Running and training has so many comparisons to our life experiences. I have had good running years and difficult ones. I have pushed forward strong and determined and have had set backs and injuries. I have run happy and run sad. I have run fast and run slow. I have run the straight and narrow, and run through hills and valleys. Satan will sense when you are tired and ready to quit and he will step back in for round 2 with thoughts like… "You are close enough, you didn't meet your time or distance goal today so you might as well stop." Punch hard with your favorite verse that reminds you of the ultimate goal (Hebrews 12:1 for me). There is NO finish line. It's step-by-step, minute by minute, hour by hour, day by day, year by year, easy courses and difficult ones, flat paths and challenging hills. When seeing the next hill, I think, "The next best moment of your life is at the top of a hill," and I push forward. John 10:10, The thief does not come except to steal, and to kill, and to destroy. I have come that they may have life, and that they have it more abundantly.

When Satan realizes that you are in it for the long run and his lies are in vain, he is down for the count, completely giving up! Then you Run for God, finishing with Him, "the author and finisher of our faith," by your side.

Cheryl Hall – Dacula, Ga.

Get in the Word

And in His name Gentiles will trust.
Matthew 12:21

The thief does not come except to steal, and to kill, and to destroy. I have come that they may have life, and that they may have it more abundantly.
John 10:10

Therefore we also, since we are surrounded by so great a cloud of witnesses, let us lay aside every weight, and the sin which so easily ensnares us, and let us run with endurance the race that is set before us, 2 looking unto Jesus, the author and finisher of our faith, who for the joy that was set before Him endured the cross, despising the shame, and has sat down at the right hand of the throne of God.
Hebrews 12:1-2

Something to Ponder

How do you defeat Satan when he wants you to give up?

What can you thank God for in EVERY run?

What is your ultimate goal for running?

Education : Injuries/Injury Prevention

Running is obviously a strenuous endeavor, and any increase in your level of activity means exposing yourself to a higher risk of injury. Once you have been running for a while, and are beginning to feel the physical benefits, the last thing you want is to be forced to stop running because of an injury. But, if you are smart, you can prevent many injuries, or at least treat them early so that they don't lead to time on the couch.

The first step in injury prevention is understanding what leads to injury. Although there are many things that can lead to injuries, there is one train of thought that covers the majority. We can call it The Terrible Toos. It means that most injuries are caused by too much of one thing or too little of another. It is important to understand that the consequences of too much of something may not be felt right away. This is the reason why we emphasize that you should run very slowly when you first begin to run, no matter how good you feel. The cumulative effect of running too hard can be devastating to your body, so by taking it easy, you avoid crossing that bridge. Another example is to never increase your weekly mileage by more than 10 percent. Too much increase in mileage will feel okay at first, but eventually will lead to breakdown. Then there are the times when too little causes problems. You can take too little time to consider and purchase the proper shoes, which can certainly lead to injury, or too little stretching could cause problems. Also, too little time spent evaluating how you feel while you run, or after you run, or ignoring symptoms, can lead you down the injury road.

The next step is to understand the difference between soreness and pain. Soreness is okay, and is an indicator that you are taxing your muscles by doing something they are not used to doing. That soreness you feel means that you are getting stronger, as long as you manage it properly. Usually, soreness is in a muscle and not a joint. Sore quadriceps, your thighs, is okay, but if the soreness is in your knee, that is not just soreness. It may be harmless, but it may be an indicator of something more serious.

Pain is usually more acute, abnormal and something that you really need to mitigate. If you have pain, and you don't change anything, it will usually get worse, so for your sake, don't ignore it. As soon as you feel pain, find a way to treat it early. When you let it go too long, it becomes a snowball rolling down a hill and is more difficult to stop with each passing day.

Of course, when in doubt, see a doctor. You can read all the research available to you, but there is no substitute for a doctor who has probably seen the condition you have and knows what is the most effective way to treat it. We will go over a number of running related injuries, but we are not suggesting that you avoid seeing your doctor.

There are some general ways to prevent injuries from hindering your progress. Here are some examples:

Running Surfaces: Running on softer surfaces, like grass or a trail, is easier on your body than concrete. Not only does it absorb shock better, but it also engages your core more than running on even surfaces. Even running on pavement is better than running on concrete. This doesn't mean that you shouldn't run if you can't find anything other than concrete sidewalks on which to run.

Shoes: Make sure you are replacing your shoes every 300 - 500 miles. This becomes more important if you are running exclusively on concrete.

Biomechanics: It is not easy to change your running form, but it is possible. Landing too hard on your heel causes more shock to your body. If you can learn to land closer to your midfoot, it will reduce those forces. And, sometimes, landing on your heel is exacerbated by a stride that is too long.

Shortening your stride will help you land more softly.

Stretching: Keeping your muscles loose will help to prevent injury. Regular stretching and massage with things like foam rollers will help to keep your muscles loose. We'll cover this more in the next chapter.

Core Strength: Take time, two or three times a week, to work on your core strength. Your core is everything from your hips to your upper abdomen. Your core stabilizes your running form and will improve your biomechanics when strengthened.

Returning from Injury: If you've had to take some time off, whether two days or two months, come back slowly and easily by decreasing distance or intensity from your regular runs. Ease your body back into regular running.

There are a number of common running related injuries. Let's get a better understanding of the definition of each, what to do about them, and how to prevent them:

Runners Knee

What is it?

Knee injuries make up about 40% of running related injuries and Patellofemoral Pain Syndrome, or Runner's Knee, makes up a majority of those. It is caused by the irritation of the cartilage at the bottom of the patella (kneecap). It usually flares up during or after a long run, while sitting for an extended period of time, or while walking downhill or down stairs. It can be caused by biomechanical issues, like over pronation, or weak core muscles leading to overstress of that area.

What to do about it?

Decrease your mileage and number of days you run. Only run as far as you can until the pain returns. Try running uphill. You put less stress on the knee and you strengthen your quads, which are both beneficial. Avoid running downhill because it will only make it worse. You can supplement your training by riding a bike, strengthening your quads, swimming or riding an elliptical machine.

How do I prevent it?

Core strengthening exercises help to correct form issues that lead to Runner's Knee, in particular, working the hips and glutes. In addition, keeping quads loose through proper stretching will reduce the knee pain. Another potential fix is to try running with a shorter stride to lessen the impact. If the pain is minor, try to use a knee strap that are available anywhere braces and wraps are sold. Just be aware that the strap will make your knee feel much better, but it does not correct the underlying problem. Continue to work on strengthening to ensure you don't have to wear that strap again in the future. Also, icing after you complete your run will help reduce inflammation. If the pain is severe, the only thing that is going to help is time off. A week off earlier is much better than a month off later!

Achilles Tendonitis

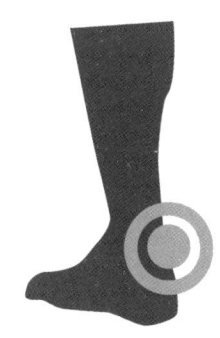

What is it?

Your calf muscles are attached to your heel via a tendon that runs from both major calf muscles to the back of your heel. When this tendon has too much pressure on it, the fibers in your tendon begin to pull away from the bone. When the fibers begin to fray, they cause inflammation, called tendonitis. It makes up a little over 10 percent of all running related injuries. It is often caused by increasing mileage or intensity and/or increasing your uphill running too much. Weak calf muscles are often another cause, or at least, a contributing factor.

What to do about it?

If you catch it early enough, you must immediately reduce the strain on the tendon by decreasing mileage, intensity and the amount of hill running you are doing. Ice the area for twenty minutes immediately following your run and another two or three times a day. If the pain is more than a nuisance, stop running. The only thing that will make achilles tendonitis better is to stop doing what caused it. When you return to running, proceed cautiously. During your downtime, you can swim or ride the elliptical machine, but cycling will probably be off-limits, as well.

How do I prevent it?

Strengthen the calf muscles by doing eccentric heel raises. Find a step, hang your heels off the back, lower your body by pulling your toes up, and then push up until you are back level with the step. Twenty of these on each leg, every day, will strengthen your calves. If you can, avoid wearing flip-flops, high heels, and aggressively stretching your calves, all of which can irritate the achilles tendon.

Shin Splints

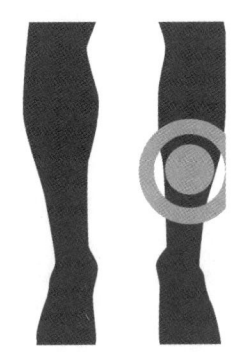

What are they?

Medial tibial stress syndrome, more commonly referred to as Shin Splints, make up almost 15 percent of running related injuries. It is caused by inflammation, or small tears of the muscles surrounding your tibia, or shinbone. This injury is most common to new runners or someone who is coming back from an extended layoff. It is an indication that you have done too much, too soon. It can also be an indication that you are wearing improper shoes or shoes with too many miles on them.

What to do about them?

As long as you catch it early, backing off your mileage, icing after running, and taking ibuprofen can reduce the inflammation. Only return to normal running after it goes away. If it is a problem with worn out or improperly fitted shoes, make a trip to a specialty-running store as soon as possible and replace your shoes. You can supplement your training with cycling or swimming.

How do I prevent them?

Only increase weekly mileage by 10 percent or less from week to week. Make sure you are in properly fitted shoes and that they have not lost cushioning due to too many miles.

Plantar Fasciitis

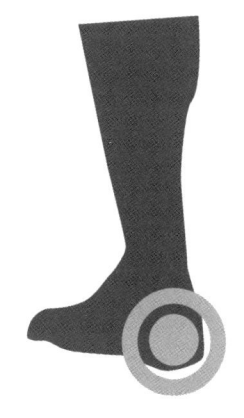

What is it?

About 15 percent of all running injuries, not surprisingly, are related to the foot. Most prevalent of those is Plantar Fasciitis, which is the inflammation or tearing away of the tendon that runs from your heel to the forefoot, usually at the heel. The pain will manifest itself from an ache to a sharp pain, sometimes in the arch, more often in the heel. It is worst first thing in the morning and makes placing your feet on the floor something to be dreaded after waking. In some cases, the physical form of your particular foot will increase the chances of Plantar Fasciitis, making preventive measures important. Also, weak core muscles, tight hip flexors or lower back issues can lead to biomechanical flaws that alter your stride just enough to cause problems in the feet. Long periods of standing on hard floors in unsupportive shoes can exacerbate the problem.

What to do about it?

Plantar Fasciitis is a notoriously difficult injury to run through and, ultimately recover from, without taking time off from running. While it is possible, it can be a chronic issue that sticks with you for a long time. You can treat it by keeping your arch loose by stretching it by either pulling your toes up gently or rolling a ball, bottle or can along the length of your arch. Even better, use a frozen water bottle and you'll ice the area at the same time. Just place the bottle, ball or can on the floor and roll your foot back and forth over it. Even taking time off will take longer than what is comfortable to most people, because you simply cannot rest it enough. Our everyday activities require us to be on our feet, which lengthen the amount of time needed for healing. Swimming is good replacement training, and you may be able to ride a bike or use an elliptical machine, but only if they do not cause significant pain.

How do I prevent it?

Once again, lack of core strength is often the underlying problem that causes just enough extra movement in the foot to result in Plantar Fasciitis. Many times, strengthening the core is all that is needed to foster healing in a case that has gone on for several years. Also, make sure your shoes are properly fitted by a specialty running store, a doctor or physical therapist. Finally, keeping your arch stretched and loose by rolling a small ball under it every day or even a couple of times a week will go a long way towards prevention.

IT (iliotibial) Band Syndrome

What is it?

The iliotibial, or IT, band runs from your hip, along the outside of your thigh, down to your knee. If you want to find it, run a roller down the outside of your thigh. When you feel that really tender band running down your leg, you have found your IT band. When you run, your knee flexes and causes the IT band to rub against the femur, the large bone in your upper leg. If you increase your mileage too quickly or increase your intensity too much, it causes irritation and inflammation. Weak muscles in your hips and glutes will lead to uncontrolled, excessive motion of the IT band, which can result in irritation. Over pronation or leg length discrepancy can also lead to problems.

What to do about it?

ITBS can be a nagging injury, but taking a day or two off and backing off your mileage for a week may alleviate the issue if you catch it early. Chances are, if you change nothing, it will get worse. Strengthen your hip muscles using side steps, side leg lifts, and/or one-legged squats. Use a foam roller down the length of your IT band to help stretch and loosen it. If over pronation is the problem, it may be time to switch to a shoe that prevents the excessive movement. Swimming or the elliptical machines are the best replacement training activities if it gets to that point. Cycling can aggravate the condition.

How can I prevent it?

The same exercises indicated above would do well to help prevent the condition. Both strengthening and lengthening will help prevent the issue from ever cropping up.

Stress Fractures

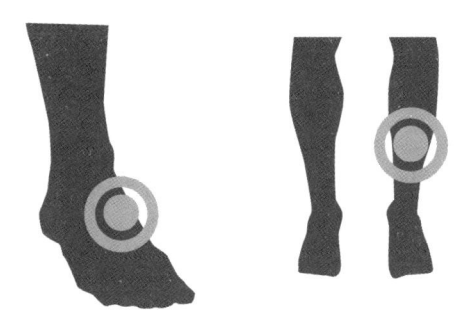

What are they?

Stress fractures are the result of cumulative trauma to a bone, unlike acute fractures, which are usually the result of a fall or blunt trauma. Runners most often have stress fractures in the tibia (shin), metatarsals (foot bones), or the calcaneus (heel) and they are one of the most serious of running injuries. The cause is usually overtraining with too little rest. The bones need time to repair themselves after each time they are traumatized. As long as you have enough rest in between each session and those sessions are not too severe, the bones can keep up, but when you don't allow enough time for repair, they break down. Stress fractures are more common in women than in men and, sometimes, nutritional deficits, low estrogen, or too little calorie intake could be contributing factors. The good news is that the more you run, over time, the stronger your bones become which lessens the likelihood of having stress fractures.

What to do about them?

Stop running. Stress fractures will not heal if you continue to run. Time off will depend upon how early you catch it, how severe the condition is, and where the fracture is located. Expect to take two to four months off from running. You may be able to walk on it (maybe not), but you cannot participate in any weight bearing activity. Swimming is the best way to maintain your fitness during the downtime.

How can I prevent them?

Weight training adds bone density, so developing a regular weight training routine would help. Also, it is important to understand that nutrition can play a significant role, so eating a balanced diet and ensuring you are getting the proper nutrients your body needs can be critical. Although it would seem like running on soft surfaces would help reduce the likelihood of stress fractures, the studies indicate that surface is not a factor in this type of injury.

Blisters

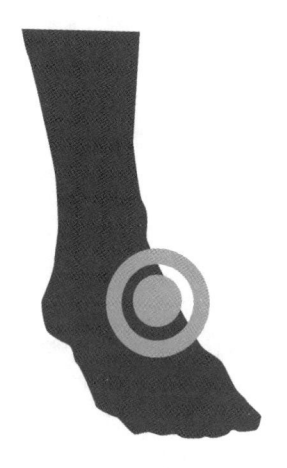

What are they?

Blisters are fluid filled sacks on the surface of your skin caused by friction between your foot and your sock and/or shoe.

What to do about them?

Small blisters (the size of a pea or less) will usually heal themselves. A larger blister may require more treatment. You should not drain a blister unless you have to due to pain, and only if you have no underlying problem that could be exacerbated by risking infection, like diabetes, for example. Blisters caused strictly by friction and not the result of another cause, like chicken pox, can be punctured using this method: Using a straight pin sterilized with alcohol, puncture a hole in the side just large enough to squeeze the liquid out. Then clean it thoroughly with soap and water. If the blister breaks on its own, wash it with soap and water. In both cases, apply an antibiotic ointment and keep it clean by applying a bandage. Replace any shoes or socks that contributed to the condition.

How can I prevent them?

A double layer of socks or a thicker sock is sometimes all you need to prevent blisters. Also, make sure your shoes are not too small and that they are made from breathable material. If you apply petroleum jelly to the areas prone to blisters prior to running, you lessen the friction.

There are certainly more running related injuries than those we have covered, but these are the most frequent. Understanding them, knowing what to look for in order to detect an injury early and being able to adjust your training appropriately is key to many years of effective running. Always consult with your doctor any time you feel something is not right. Be careful with research on the Internet, too. Although there is a wealth of information there, sometimes you can be steered in the wrong direction.

Whether we are sore from working extra hard, or have some type of injury, we can take comfort in this verse:

And God will wipe away every tear from their eyes; there shall be no more death, nor sorrow, nor crying. There shall be no more pain, for the former things have passed away. Revelation 21:4

Someday, if you are a child of the King, there will be no injuries!

Quote of the Week

"A pessimist sees the difficulty in every opportunity; an optimist sees the opportunity in every difficulty." Winston Churchill

Workout Journal

Week 4

Workout #1, 2, and 3

Start with a brisk 5-minute warm-up walk.
Jog 90 Seconds
Walk 90 Seconds
Jog 3 Minutes
Walk 3 Minutes
Jog 90 Seconds
Walk 90 Seconds
Jog 3 Minutes
Walk 3 Minutes
5 minute cool-down walk.

Total Workout = 28 Minutes

Be sure to download The 5K Challenge App which can be found in your app store.

Workout #1

Date _____Distance _____Time _____

Notes _____

_____

Weather _____

Workout #2

Date _____Distance _____Time _____

Notes _____

_____

Weather _____

Workout #3

Date _____Distance _____Time _____

Notes _____

_____

Weather _____

Stretching / Core

Week 5

Take Personal Inventory

What are my goals for this week?
_____
_____
_____
_____

What are the things that I need to pray for this week?
_____
_____
_____
_____

What are the challenges that potentially lay ahead this week?
_____
_____
_____
_____

Reflect back on the past week and take inventory. What went right? What went wrong? What were some of the highlights? Be specific.

Week 5 : Streching / Core and Hurry

Week 5 : Streching / Core and Hurry

Main Story : "The Hurrier I Go, the Behinder I Get." Lewis Caroll

When three of my Run for God graduates ran their first 5K this past year, their excitement ran high as they took their places at the starting line. This was the culmination of 12 weeks of training for their very first 5K and they were ready to run! When the gun went off they stayed together for the first mile. At mile two, they were still within sight of each other, but when they hit mile three, that was no longer the case. As they crossed the finish line, all at different times, you could see the smiles on their faces, proud that they had accomplished their goal of running their very first 5K.

Later, one of the participants who fell behind the others said to me, "It seemed like I was going so fast, and up ahead, you all looked like you were moving in slow motion. I thought, 'I can surely catch up!' But instead, the faster I tried to go, the further you all moved ahead, until I could no longer see any of you anymore." It was clear that she felt disappointment in not being able to keep up with her fellow Run for God classmates. I could relate to her statement, because I too, have started a race with the intention of keeping up with another runner or at least keeping that person in my view. At some point, though, I usually lost sight of them and didn't see them again until the end of the race.

In life, we do the same thing. We try to keep up. But who and what are we trying to keep up with? Are we trying to keep up appearances? We all want to present our best self to others, right? Are we trying to keep up with some ideal of perfection and afraid we'll look bad if we end up at the back of the pack? Or, are we trying to keep up a lifestyle that consumes all our time and energy so that we can have material possessions? The danger in playing the "keep up" game is that as soon as we fall behind, we begin to feel frustrated and deflated. We begin to wonder, "What's wrong with me? Why can't I keep up?" But maybe our perspective is a little skewed. To my RFG runner, it appeared to her that the others were moving in slow motion, making it seem as if running was much easier for her running friends up ahead. Once everyone crossed the finish line, however, and shared their stories, it was apparent that each runner was struggling to some extent in keeping up his/her race pace. One's perspective does not always reflect re ality. It may appear that others seem to have an easier road to travel, when in fact, that is far from the truth.

During our 12-week class, participants were reminded frequently to run their own race and not compare themselves to others, unless the comparison motivated and inspired them to improve. Under those circumstances, emulation can be a good thing. The downside of comparing ourselves to others is that we diminish our own successes and accomplishments, beating ourselves up to the point that we feel like utter failures sometimes. More importantly, we diminish who we are in God's eyes. Psalm 139:13-16, For You formed my inward parts; You covered me in my mother's womb. I will praise You, for I am fearfully and wonderfully made; Marvelous are Your works, And that my soul knows very well. My frame was not hidden from You, When I was made in secret, And skillfully wrought in the lowest parts of the earth. Your eyes saw my substance, being yet unformed. And in Your book they all were written, The days fashioned for me, When as yet there were none of them.

We should celebrate that there is no one else like us, that God uniquely designed each of us for His purpose. We should also acknowledge that, without GOD, we can do NOTHING. In fact, we are blessed to simply be in the race. For future races, I encouraged my class to always remember that the race is not about them. It's about God and running His race with Grace. It doesn't matter how many cross the finish line in front of you. What matters is that you cross it, look up, and smile, thanking the One who enabled you to experience the journey. Proverbs 4:25-26, Let your eyes look straight ahead, And your eyelids look right before you. 26 Ponder the path of your feet, And let all your ways be established. Do not be distracted by faster runners.

You're not called to do what everyone else is doing. You are called to live a life for GOD and to run YOUR race for Him. Ever since my first 5K experience in 2003 in which I finished dead last, my mantra has been "The race is not always to the swift but to those who keep on running." 15 years later, God has blessed and empowered me to run 65 long distance events, including 59 half marathons, 2 23Ks, 2 25Ks, and 2 50Ks, turning 65 years of age along the way.

He has also blessed me with leading Run for God classes since 2012. Matthew 24:13, But he who endures to the end shall be saved. Just as running takes dedication and discipline, so does our relationship with God. If we remember Whom we belong to and use our God-given abilities to serve and glorify Him, there's no one who can steal our joy. There's no stopping us in getting to that finish line.

Linda Null – Wappapello, MO

Get in the Word

For You formed my inward parts; You covered me in my mother's womb. I will praise You, for I am fearfully and wonderfully made; Marvelous are Your works, And that my soul knows very well. My frame was not hidden from You, When I was made in secret, And skillfully wrought in the lowest parts of the earth. Your eyes saw my substance, being yet unformed. And in Your book they all were written, The days fashioned for me, When as yet there were none of them. Psalm 139:13-16

Let your eyes look straight ahead, And your eyelids look right before you. 26 Ponder the path of your feet, And let all your ways be established. Proverbs 4:25-26

But he who endures to the end shall be saved. Matthew 24:13

Something to Ponder

What are some things in life you struggle to keep up with?

_____

What can you do when you fall behind so that you don't lose hope and give up?

_____

Are you living YOUR life or are you trying to live someone else's life?

_____

Education : Stretching / Core

There is a lot of controversy over the issue of stretching, mostly related to the timing and type of stretching we do. The studies have made two things very clear: 1) You should never stretch cold muscles. It is important to warm muscles up before beginning any type of stretches. 2) Other than attempting to stretch cold muscles, you won't do any harm stretching. At worst, you may be spending time doing something that doesn't have big benefits. One other conclusion that you will find in most studies is that stretching is more beneficial after you run than before you run.

The water is a little more murky when it comes to the type of stretching you choose to do. There are many types, but we will discuss the three most popular; Static, Active and Dynamic. Of those, we will provide examples for Static stretching. As the name suggests, this category has the runner in positions that are held for fifteen to thirty seconds, which allows muscles to slowly lengthen while the position is held. In contrast, Active and Dynamic stretches use motion to help stretch and lengthen the muscles.

As we go through each stretch, keep these things in mind: 1) Stretching should not hurt. You should feel the area being stretched, but if it hurts, it is an indication of an underlying problem. 2) Only stretch far enough to feel it. Pushing stretches too far can lead to injury. 3) Hold each stretch for fifteen to thirty seconds. 4) Position is very important! Place yourself in exactly the position indicated. Changing your position changes the area you are stretching, which is not optimal. 5) Stretching before an easy run may or may not help. The two most critical times to stretch are before running fast in a workout or a race, and after you run. 6) These stretches can be done indoors or outdoors. They are most comfortable on a soft, but firm surface, like grass.

We will share seven stretches that will work the major running muscle groups. There are certainly many stretches that will help you to stretch other, more minor, muscle groups. If you find that you have particularly tight areas, the resources are almost endless. Don't be afraid to research and find what works best for you. The stretches we are sharing may not be, necessarily, the best stretches for you, but they are solid, time tested basic stretches.

Week 5 : Streching / Core and Hurry

Hang Stretch

As the name suggests, keeping your feet together, simply bend at the waist and let the weight of your upper body pull you towards your toes. If you can touch your toes by allowing your body to use gravity, great. If you are nowhere close to your toes, don't worry about it. Do not force yourself down to your toes. Keep your legs straight. If you are doing it right, you will notice that, as you relax and the muscles begin to stretch, you will move a couple of inches closer to the floor as you hold the position. This will only happen if you are properly relaxed and not forcing your weight down.

Grab your Heels

While you are still in the hang stretch position and you have completed the time for your Hang stretch, reach and grab your heels by bending your knees and pulling your face towards your knees. Now try to gently straighten your legs. You should feel the intensity in your hamstrings and glutes increase. Most people cannot fully straighten their legs. It is easy to lose your balance at this point, so be careful. As you come out of this stretch, do it slowly, arching your back as you get back to a standing position.

Lunge Stretch

As the name suggests, this is very much like performing lunges. From the position you finished the last stretch, take a very large step forward and place your hands on the ground in front of you. Your front leg should be perpendicular (90 degrees) to the ground and your hands should be on the inside of your knee with your shoulder right next to your knee. Your trailing foot should be bent with the ball of your foot on the ground. From this position, push your hips towards the ground so that your trailing knee is close to the ground, but not touching it. You should feel the stretch all along the inside of your hamstring on the front leg and through your hip and inside of your quads on your trailing leg. This stretch may be difficult for some to hold more than twenty seconds. Don't forget to stretch both sides.

Groin Stretch

While you are still on the ground, begin the next stretch by getting on your hands and knees with your arms and legs perpendicular to the ground, and then move one leg so that you stretch it out to the side as far as you can, straightening your leg fully. Now place the foot of your stretched out leg flat on the ground and point your toes forward so that your foot is parallel to your body. You should feel this stretch along your groin and the inside of your leg, as well as the outside, lower part of the leg from knee to ankle. You will need to switch and stretch both sides.

Week 5 : Streching / Core and Hurry

Butterfly

Now sit straight up on your rear end and bend both knees to bring the soles of both your feet together so that they are flat against each other. Now pull both feet towards your body as far as you can, pulling them in with your hands, and gently move your knees down towards the ground. Keep your hands on your feet. Do not bounce.

Flamingo Stretch (Quad Stretch)

From a standing position with your feet together, bend one of your legs as far as you can and grab the foot with your hand (from the same side of your body), pulling it behind you until it is resting against the glute. Your knees should be together. You should feel this in your quads. You may need something to hold onto with the other hand to maintain balance. Remember to do both legs.

Calf Stretch

Find a wall, a post, a fence, or some other stationary object, and lean against it with your foot a few feet from the object. Keeping one of your legs straight, lean against the wall, but keep your heel on the ground. Your foot should be pointed directly at the object you are using for support. Use your other foot for stability by placing it forward under you.

Core Exercises

Your core is comprised of your abs, oblique's, lower back, glutes and all the muscles around your hips. Keeping these muscles strong will make your running more enjoyable and free from injury. Why? Your core will stabilize everything else around it, and strengthening it will help you run with better form. Many injuries are caused by a flaw in form that is repeated thousands of times and, eventually, leads to overuse and consequent injury. Running with better form is important to avoid injury, and core strength is essential to good form.

Runners are notorious for skipping the core work, even though many know the benefits it provides. We all know that running makes us better runners, right? Duh! So we spend all of our time running because we don't have time for the things that may complement it, or do we? Sure it may be difficult to find time, but you don't have to spend a lot of time doing core exercises to see a big benefit. Make it a part of what you do by scheduling it in along with your runs. A five or ten minute core routine after you complete your run will not add too much time, but it will be worth it. Although it is best to do core work after you run, it is not necessary. Another good time to do core work might be while you are watching television. You can get down on the floor while the news is on and accomplish a lot. Be creative and find some time when you can strengthen your core. It will pay off.

There are hundreds, if not thousands, of core exercises. A simple Internet search will produce thousands of results, but we will focus on the proverbial tip of the iceberg, focusing on getting the core muscles stronger by using seven exercises.

Week 5 : Streching / Core and Hurry

Plank

Due to its effectiveness, the Plank is a very popular exercise. Most people can do planks, but the amount of time spent in this position varies greatly. Simply lie on the floor face down and push up to place your weight on your feet and elbows while maintaining a straight line down the length of your body. Hold this position for thirty seconds to a minute. Do this three to five times.

Side Plank

The side plank is a much more difficult exercise for most people. Again, the idea is to hold your body in a straight line, only this time, balance your weight on one elbow and the side of one foot. If you cannot perform this exercise, don't fret. Keep trying, and as you strengthen your core, you can work your way up to do these!

Bridge

Lie on your back and bend your knees so that your feet are flat on the floor. Pick your hips off the floor so that you are on your upper back and feet, but your lower back and hips are off the floor. Place your body in a straight line from your shoulders to your knees. Hold this position for ten seconds, relax, and repeat ten times.

Donkey Kicks

Get down on your hands and knees so that your arms and legs are perpendicular to the floor. Pick up one of your knees and thrust your foot back and up, away from the floor. Bring your knee back down towards the floor. Do three sets of ten on each leg.

Squats

Place your feet a little wider than shoulder width. Bending at the waist and the knees, keep your back straight, and squat down as if you are about to sit on a bench. Drop down low enough to make your thighs parallel with the floor, and then raise back up. Do these in a slow, controlled motion. Do three sets of ten.

Lateral Leg Raises

Stand with your feet together near a stationary object. Use the object to stabilize yourself and lift your leg directly to the side. Push your leg out as far as you can in a motion that is not slow or fast, but controlled. Let your leg back down. Do three sets of ten on each leg.

Week 5 : Streching / Core and Hurry

Hip Hikes

This works best if you can find a step to work on. Stand sideways so that one foot is off the side of the step. Allow your foot to drop below the top of the step and then lift it as high as you can, keeping your legs straight, tilting your hips to make the motion happen. Again, do three sets of ten on each leg.

If you are not able to do some of these exercises, do the ones you can. As you become stronger and you continue to run, they will become easier. Likewise, if you can only do one set of each, that's fine. Just begin to build the habit of core strengthening while you are getting started as a runner. It will make your running even more fruitful!

Be sober, be vigilant; because your adversary the devil walks about like a roaring lion, seeking whom he may devour. Resist him, steadfast in the faith, knowing that the same sufferings are experienced by your brotherhood in the world. 1 Peter 5:8-9

Some translations read, "Be well balanced." Satan is looking to keep you on the couch. Whether we stay on the couch because we lack the willpower to get out the door and exercise, or because we are injured because we weren't "well balanced," we let him win the battle. Be vigilant against your adversary, whether it is spiritually against the devil, or physically against idleness!

Quote of the Week

"Always bear in mind that your own resolution to succeed is more important than any other one thing." Abraham Lincoln

Notes

Week 5 : Streching / Core and Hurry

Notes

Workout Journal

Week 5

Workout #1, 2, and 3

Start with a brisk 5-minute warm-up walk.
Jog 3 Minutes
Walk 90 Seconds
Jog 5 Minutes
Walk 2 Minutes
Jog 3 Minutes
Walk 90 Seconds
Jog 5 Minutes
Walk 3 Minutes
5 minute cool-down walk.

Total Workout = 34 Minutes

Be sure to download The 5K Challenge App which can be found in your app store.

Workout #1

Date _____ Distance _____ Time _____

Notes _____

_____

Weather _____

Workout #2

Date _____ Distance _____ Time _____

Notes _____

_____

Weather _____

Workout #3

Date _____ Distance _____ Time _____

Notes _____

_____

Weather _____

Weight Loss
Misconceptions

Week 6

Take Personal Inventory

What are my goals for this week?
_____
_____
_____
_____

What are the things that I need to pray for this week?
_____
_____
_____
_____

What are the challenges that potentially lay ahead this week?
_____
_____
_____
_____

Reflect back on the past week and take inventory. What went right? What went wrong? What were some of the highlights? Be specific.

Week 6 : Weight Loss and The Turning Point

Main Story : The Turning Point

I am a general dentist in Ohio. I have been practicing for 41 years, mainly doing oral surgeries: bone grafting and dental implants. Since I do medical histories every day, I am keenly aware of the general health status of my population of patients. About 5 years ago, I began to realize that Americans were getting sicker and sicker. Cardiovascular disease, diabetes, cancer, multiple sclerosis, kidney failure, rheumatoid arthritis, lupus, and many other health issues were running rampant. Obesity, not just being overweight, was getting much more common. It was not unusual for my patients to be on 7-10 different medications per day. Bypass surgeries and stent placements were becoming the norm. What was going on? Why was our healthcare system failing us? I prayed that God would give me a clue. He did.

I stumbled upon a movie called "Forks Over Knives". Ah, ha......it's in the food! It led me down the path of daily studying about nutrition and health and how diseases work. I learned from the folks who did this research. They were all telling the same story; we don't have to be a sick culture. I began a whole-food, plant-based diet. It felt so right, and the daily research that I studied confirmed that I was on the right track. But I was lacking a key component to my health: exercise.

I like to run, but I only did it sporadically. I could not seem to motivate myself. Then along came Run For God at my church, Hope Church in Brunswick. Now I had a goal, a team, and motivation. Now I was running not just for myself but also for God. I was running last night in Week 9 of the program and realized that I was filled with the Holy Spirit. Here I was, almost 67 years old, running with absolutely nothing hurting - feeling powerful. I am on no medication, only slightly overweight, have excellent blood pressure, and a resting heart rate that is getting better every week. God gave me the Run For God program - the missing piece for me. Now my lifestyle is all His. He created our bodies - His Temples - as the most amazing machines known to man, and He is so glad that I am finally truly taking care of mine. I am not only running for Him. I am running to Him.

Week 6 : Weight Loss and The Turning Point

Dr. Daniel P. Camm DDS - Brunswick, Ohio

Get in the Word

Or do you not know that your body is the temple of the Holy Spirit who is in you, whom you have from God, and you are not your own? For you were bought at a price; therefore glorify God in your body and in your spirit, which are God's.
1Corinthians 6:19-20

Therefore we do not lose heart. Though outwardly we are wasting away, yet inwardly we are being renewed day by day. For our light and momentary troubles are achieving for us an eternal glory that far outweighs them all. So we fix our eyes not on what is seen, but on what is unseen, since what is seen is temporary, but what is unseen is eternal.
2Corinthians 4:15-18

I have fought the good fight, I have finished the race, I have kept the faith. Finally, there is laid up for me the crown of righteousness, which the Lord, the righteous Judge, will give to me on that Day, and not to me only but also to all who have loved His appearing.
2Timothy 4:7-8

Something to Ponder

There were two trees in the Garden of Eden. We chose the wrong tree, and it has made all the difference. How does our gaining the Tree of the Knowledge of Good and Evil affect how we take care of our bodies?

Americans use 25% of the world resources for our indulgent pleasure, wanting to have as much as possible with the least expenditure of energy. How does Running for God change your attitude about that?

What foods can give you the energy you need for your running journey?

Education : Weight Loss Misconceptions

Losing weight is one of the chief motivators for beginning and/or maintaining any running program. It may not be that every runner wants to lose weight, but the percentage of those who do is high, especially among beginners. There is a tremendous amount of information available today, and access to it has never been easier. But not all information is created equal. Some is good, and some is bad. How do you know what to take to heart and what to let go? Let's go over common misconceptions about weight loss. In general, keep in mind that anything absolute is usually not best for you. For example, I know people who will eat no bread because they are convinced it will lead to weight gain. Cutting back on bread may be good for you, but cutting it out completely is probably not the way to go. There are many examples of diets like this. Be suspicious of any diet that doesn't offer a balanced approach. This brings us to our first weight loss misconception:

Fad diets work.

Fad diets will often lead to rapid weight loss, which is not necessarily good for you. And once you have lost the weight, the diet is impossible to continue due to the strict nature of most fad diets. Cutting out entire food groups, or limiting calorie intake too much may produce results for a time, but they can cause shortages in your body of important nutrients that can lead to health issues down the road. What happens when you have lost the weight you wanted to lose? Typically, you pick back up with the eating habits you had before the diet and the weight comes back.

Skipping meals will help you lose weight.

Skipping meals only serves to make you hungrier later and leads to overeating at the next meal. By eating three meals a day, in addition to healthy snacks in between, your blood sugar stabilizes and your body continues to burn calories all day. Try smaller meals instead of cutting them out completely.

What you eat matters more than how much.

The key word is moderation. Too much of anything can lead to weight gain. Both quantity and quality matter. For example, a bagel would seem to be a better alternative to a doughnut hole, but the bagel has many more calories. Limiting quantity can be just as important as what you eat.

The lower the calories, the faster you will lose weight.

This is one of the biggest mistakes I see. While it is true that weight loss is all about calories in versus calories burned, your body is more complex than that. If you limit your calorie intake too much, your body goes into "starvation mode" and it learns to live on fewer calories by slowing your metabolism while storing more fat for reserves in the future. This is the chief reason why losing about one pound a week is ideal. If you are losing more, you could be teaching your body to live on too few calories.

Eating healthy costs too much.

I hear this all the time. "I would love to eat healthy, but it is too expensive." Eating healthy does not have to be expensive. One of the biggest myths is that fresh vegetables are the only healthy way to eat them, but fresh spinach, for example, and canned spinach contain the same nutrients. You can eat canned and frozen vegetables if you educate yourself a little about reading labels. Look for low sodium foods packed in water or their own juices. Remember to rinse canned vegetables out of the can to rid it of excess salt. Canned tuna packed in water is a low cost, low fat food that can be stored for long periods of time.

Desserts are forbidden.

There is room in your diet for any kind of food, especially the ones you love the most. Of course, limiting the portions and the number of times you eat them is critical. Trying to completely cut out foods that you love will often lead to binge eating and, ultimately, discouragement. Just limit your caloric intake.

You don't have to diet if you exercise.

Both are important factors in the weight loss cycle. While it is almost as simple as calories in versus calories burned, you may be hungrier from the increased activity. If you're not careful, you can replace the burned calories with even more calories consumed. You have to monitor both to successfully lose weight.

Don't snack between meals.

Snacking between meals is actually a good idea, as long as the snacks are healthy and you limit the quantity. Eating smaller meals five or six times a day will keep your metabolism rate higher and will lessen the cravings you get when you are hungry since you are satisfying them more often. Part of the reason snacking gets such a bad name is that candy bars and potato chips are the foods we tend to associate with snack time. Make sure that you are choosing healthy alternatives for in between meals.

You have to eat breakfast to lose weight.

Let me preface this by saying that you should eat breakfast to get your metabolism up and running early. However, a study by the American Journal of Clinical Nutrition showed that it doesn't make a difference when all other factors are the same and overall food intake is the same. The point is that if you have to skip breakfast on occasion because of time constraints, it will not cause you to gain weight. Just know that you will be very hungry by your next meal and you will need to be careful to not overeat.

Eating meat will make me gain weight.

It is a fact that, on average, vegetarians have lower body mass index than meat eaters, but you have to dig a little deeper to find the reasoning. Vegetarians are more likely to be at a healthy weight because they limit their calorie intake. You can choose to eat meat and limit your calories and you can successfully maintain a healthy body weight. Both choices can be healthy!

Starches are fattening and should always be avoided.

Foods such as bread, rice, pasta, cereals, beans, fruits and some vegetables are high in starch, but are low in fat. They only become bad for you when eaten in large portion sizes or with high-fat toppings like butter, sour cream, or mayonnaise. These foods are an important source of energy for your body. Choose healthier alternatives like whole wheat bread, brown rice, oatmeal, or bran cereals. Other foods, like beans, peas, and vegetables are starchy but are high in dietary fiber too.

Cut out all sweets.

It is great advice to cut out sweets when you are trying to lose weight because they tend to be high in calories. However, you can have your cake and eat it too. Once again, when you cut out a food that you really like, you set yourself up for failure. If you eventually fall into the trap of eating that chocolate cake, you will eat too much. It is more effective, for most people, to eat the occasional small helping of sweets. Just remember, those calories count. It is worth noting that some people have the ability to cut out foods like this and not crave them. That is the best alternative, but if you fall into the majority who don't have that kind of willpower, it is wiser to eat the occasional sweet treat in moderation.

Bread is bad.

See the section on Starches.

Chocolate makes you fat.

Dark chocolate is full of antioxidants and may increase your HDL cholesterol (good), while decreasing your LDL cholesterol (bad). If you eat sweets, a calorie is a calorie, so whether it is chocolate or anything else, they have the same effect on your body. See the section about cutting out all sweets.

Eating more fruits and vegetables will help you lose weight.

If you only add fruits and vegetables to your diet and expect to lose weight as a result, you will be disappointed. All you are doing is adding calories and isn't that opposite from our goal? Instead, replace your high calorie foods with fruits and vegetables to decrease the total amount of calories you are consuming. You will also be getting necessary fiber, vitamins and minerals!

You should never eat fast food.

Fast foods should never be your primary source of food, but if you make smart choices, you can eat reasonable meals and still lose weight. Avoid large portions. Choose water over soda. Instead of eating french fries, most places offer alternatives, like salads or fruits. Pick grilled chicken and avoid fried foods. Eschew the high fat toppings like mayonnaise, high fat salad dressings, bacon, and cheese.

Don't eat late.

This one is partially true. You want to avoid eating right before you go to bed because you won't have time for your body to begin to burn it off, but eating a sensible snack in the evening is okay as long as it keeps you within your calorie limit for the day. Many times, eating in the evening turns into binge eating something you have been craving all day. If this is you, limit your quantities by taking a small portion and leaving the rest in the refrigerator or cabinet.

Don't weigh yourself often.

Many diets propose that you only weigh yourself periodically because the daily fluctuations of your weight can be discouraging. No one likes to see a higher number today than yesterday, but constant vigilance can also provide motivation. It is just as easy to look at the higher number and be motivated to do better today as it is to be discouraged by it. If you prepare for it and choose how you will react before seeing it, you are more likely to be motivated. It all comes down to preference and personality. If you can handle it, knowing your daily number helps to keep your focus.

There is such a thing as negative calorie foods.

Once again, this one is true, but be careful. Negative calorie foods are those foods that require more energy to digest than the amount of energy in the item itself. The net effect is that you burn more calories than you consume. While these foods, such as celery, apples, pickles, grapefruit and more are healthy choices; they do come with some calorie content. You are safe to eat as much of these foods as you like, but don't forget to count them. We get into trouble when we look at fat free and sugar free foods the same way we look at negative calorie foods. Most of these foods are either not calorie free or have no nutritional value. Focus on foods that have nutritional value that stay within your calorie intake allowance for weight loss.

Lifting weights will make me bulk up.

Lifting weights or doing other strength training activities on a regular basis can help you lose weight. These activities build muscle, and muscle burns more calories than body fat. If you have more muscle, you burn more calories, even sitting still! Contrary to popular thought, strengthening activities will not "bulk you up." Only the most intense strength training and certain genetic backgrounds are ingredients for building very large muscles.

You have to lose a lot of weight to make a difference.

Weight loss is weight loss. The closer you get to your ideal weight, the better, but small improvements can have the biggest impact on your health. Losing five to ten pounds can have a positive impact on blood pressure, for example. Not to mention the lower impact on your body as you run!

Weight loss comes down to how much you put in versus how much you burn, but the quality of those calories is important too. Just remember that losing weight is not something you do overnight. It takes effort and smart, conscious choices. If you fail to make the best choices today, it doesn't have to mean that you give up.

Romans 3:23 says, *"For all have sinned and fall short of the glory of God."*

We make mistakes because we are wired that way. Dieting is no different than anything else we do in life, but just because we have a fender-bender, get a ticket, or accidentally cut someone off in traffic, doesn't mean we quit driving. When we stumble, we get back on track. After all, the Bible also says in Philippians 4:13, *"I can do all things through Christ who strengthens me."*

Quote of the Week

"I enjoy few things more than making people smile." S. Truett Cathy

Notes

Week 6 : Weight Loss and The Turning Point

Notes

Workout Journal

Week 6

Workout #1, 2, and 3

Start with a brisk 5-minute warm-up walk.
Jog 3 Minutes
Walk 90 Seconds
Jog 5 Minutes
Walk 2 Minutes
Jog 3 Minutes
Walk 90 Seconds
Jog 5 Minutes
Walk 3 Minutes
5 minute cool-down walk.

Total Workout = 34 Minutes

Be sure to download The 5K Challenge App which can be found in your app store.

Workout #1

Date _____ Distance _____ Time _____

Notes _____

_____

Weather _____

Workout #2

Date _____ Distance _____ Time _____

Notes _____

_____

Weather _____

Workout #3

Date _____ Distance _____ Time _____

Notes _____

_____

Weather _____

Motivation

Week 7

Take Personal Inventory

What are my goals for this week?
_____
_____
_____
_____

What are the things that I need to pray for this week?
_____
_____
_____
_____

What are the challenges that potentially lay ahead this week?
_____
_____
_____
_____

Reflect back on the past week and take inventory. What went right? What went wrong? What were some of the highlights? Be specific.

Week 7 : Motivation and Jesus Wept

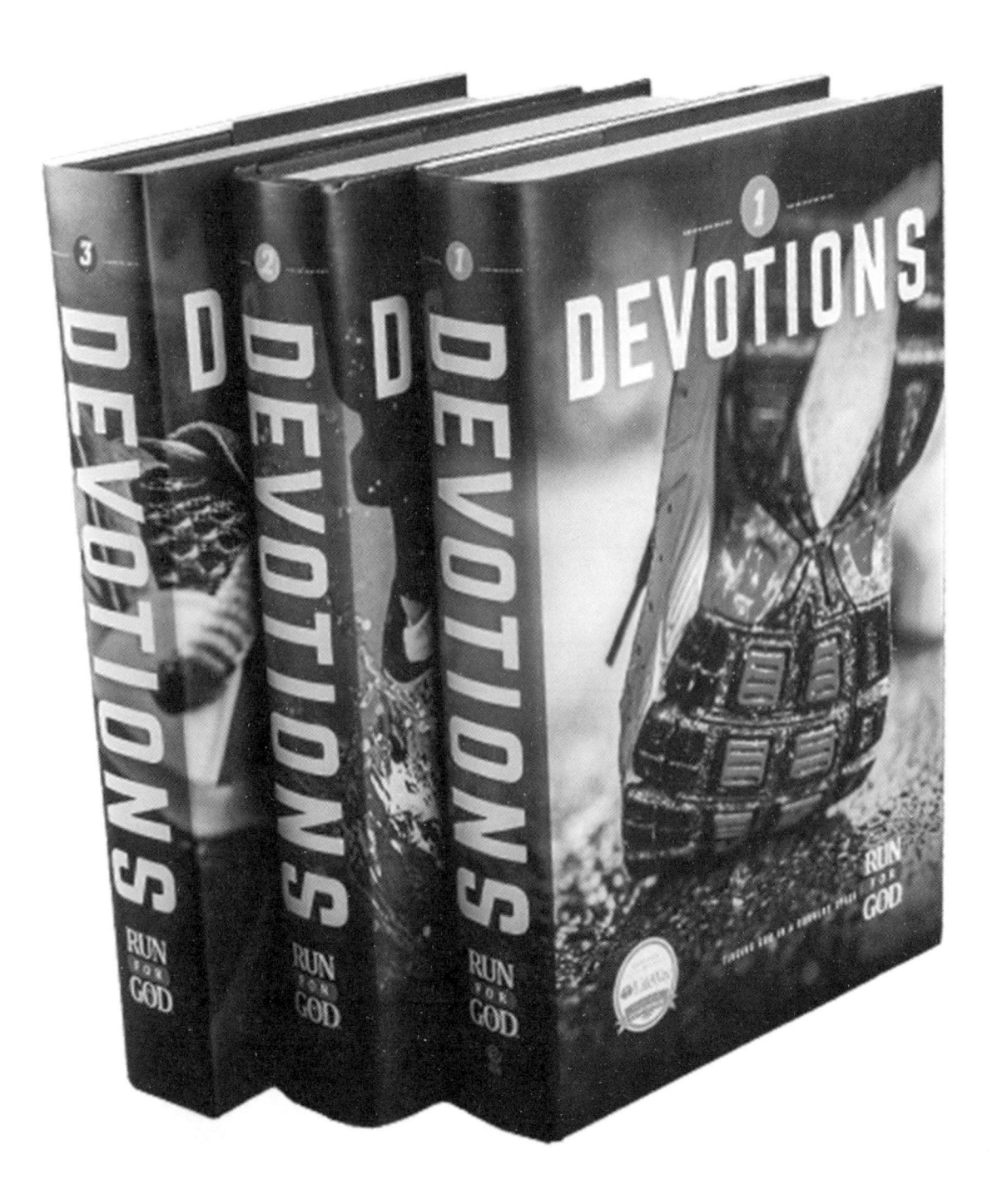

Week 7 : Motivation and Jesus Wept

Main Story : Jesus Wept. It's not just the shortest verse.

Jesus wept. John 11:35 As a former elementary school teacher in a Christian school, I admit I used to joke about that notable verse in the Bible. It is said to be famous for being the shortest verse. Students would remind me of this fact when it was time for those long Scripture memorization quizzes. One year I thought about assigning that verse…on April 1st. I've never been good at memorizing. When I had to give presentations in school or at work, I literally wrote out what I wanted to say verbatim for fear that if I forgot something, I'd veer treacherously off track.

When I was a sophomore in high school and introduced to a dynamic, loving church youth group, it was there that I first opened a Bible. I had no clue how to go about "reading" the Bible much less how to use one for its intended purpose of knowing God better. I'm not sure when exactly I got it in my head that I needed to memorize Scripture. It seemed like everyone at church could quote verses and even use them in meaningful, encouraging ways. Fast forward thirty-five years…

I'm still bad at memorizing things of significant length. But with regards to the truly important stuff, God has used running as the most effective memorization tool. After all, one simply cannot tote around notes or a big heavy Bible whilst running. So, He went one step better and gave me His Holy Spirit to remind me at the most critical, opportune moments of key points from His Word: *But the Helper, the Holy Spirit, whom the Father will send in My name, He will teach you all things, and bring to your remembrance all things that I said to you. John 14:26*

Last week's hill training run is a good example. As soon as I hit the first big hill, I heard footsteps behind me. Those footsteps quickly materialized into several young men in blue fire department shirts and shorts holding giant yellow walkie-talkies. It crossed my mind for a split second to try to keep their pace. Then I heard laughter. No, it wasn't coming from those strapping young firemen. It was coming from common sense. As they blew past me on their own training run, I was humbled as I pictured them in full gear and oxygen tanks running into a burning forest or building risking their own lives to potentially save one. With this image in my head, I prayed for their safety. Verses about God's hand of protection came to mind. The rest of that day's hill run was filled with more prayers as God kept bringing people and situations to mind. Verses about continual, persistent prayer, persevering through trials, putting on the full armor of God, courage over fear, peace, strength, and healing accompanied each step and breath. I couldn't stop. At one point, it felt like my heart would burst from being reminded of so many people that needed prayer. It felt like each person was not only on my mind but now flooding my heart.

There are times I cry out "God, how do you handle all this? I can't even take the few you've placed on my heart today, yet you know and hear the cries of seven billion of us all at once!" Humbling for sure. Funny thing about being humbled. It's actually a good place to be since THIS is how God can best reach us. Perhaps this is why when I'm running I can hear God so clearly. Running has humbled me more often and more consistently than anything else. Check in on me at Mile 20 of any marathon and you'll see. I used to think the definition of being humble was self-degradation: "I'll never be as good as so-and-so." "I'm not worthy of that promotion." "Why would anyone like me?" Years ago, I heard or read – can't remember where – the definition of humble as "knowing who you are in relation to God." I've also heard it put as "seeing yourself as God sees you."

On that hill run, one verse kept coming to mind which I don't usually share because I used to think it wouldn't be very humble of me to do so. It was from James 5:16 The effective, fervent prayer of a righteous man avails much. I realize I have hesitated to share this verse for fear of coming across as arrogant or boastful. It is because of one word in the verse: righteous. I even "version-surfed" to see if there was a more palatable word, but most still say "righteous." Knowing that I was wrong about the word "humble," I had to look up the word "righteous" and debunk my previous mindset of the association with the term "self-righteous." Turns out that humble and righteous kind of go hand-in-hand as I found these versions of the same verse: "The prayer of a person living right with God is something powerful to be reckoned with." "When a believing person prays, great things happen." Okay, who among us wouldn't want their prayers to be powerful and produce great things?

This year God used my emotions and tears to bring relevance to the verse I used to skim over and even joked about. "Jesus wept." It comes from the passage in Scripture detailing the death of Lazarus, brother of Mary and

Martha. You don't need to be a Bible scholar to know that this is the famous "raising Lazarus from the tomb" account. It's even become a household football term used when a team or player miraculously pulls out a win or resurrects a career against all circumstances and odds. But I digress. What I never paid attention to before was the moment when Jesus actually wept. When Jesus saw her weeping, and the Jews who had come along with her also weeping, he was deeply moved in spirit and troubled. "Where have you laid him?" He asked, "Come and see, Lord," they replied. Jesus wept. Then the Jews said, "See how He loved him!" John 11:33-36 But why then? After all, Lazarus had already been dead four days when Jesus finally arrived at Mary and Martha's home. He had already received the news before then. Plus, being the Son of God and all, He already knew he was going to raise Lazarus from the tomb and there would be a happy ending.

So why did He cry when He did? Or at all? I'm no Bible scholar and still feel uncomfortable using the words humble and righteous, but I think Jesus wept at that precise moment for me to know how much I am loved. He wants me to know that He not only sees my tears but also feels them Himself. Why is this important? I believe it is crucial in my faith that He can and will answer my prayers. And that He will do so in ways that undeniably prove He was there when I was crying. It brings me to tears when I think about the lengths He goes to so that I know the depth of His love.

Irene Tang – Pleasanton, CA

Get in the Word

But the Helper, the Holy Spirit, whom the Father will send in My name, He will teach you all things, and bring to your remembrance all things that I said to you.
John 14:26

The effective, fervent prayer of a righteous man avails much
James 5:16

Therefore, when Jesus saw her weeping, and the Jews who came with her weeping, He groaned in the spirit and was troubled. And He said, "Where have you laid him?" They said to Him, "Lord, come and see." Jesus wept. Then the Jews said, "See how He loved him! John 11:33-36

Something to Ponder

What methods, strategies, or teaching tips help you learn best? If you find memorizing Scripture challenging, take a moment to write down a few ways you can incorporate "best learning practices" with verses.

_____

_____

Do you feel your prayers are powerful and effective?

_____

_____

When was the last time you cried? Do you believe Jesus was there crying with you? How does that belief impact your faith in your relationship with God?

_____

_____

Week 7 : Motivation and Jesus Wept

Education : Motivation, Yes you CAN!

Probably, the number one reason people have difficulty getting outdoors to run is time. We're all busy, and finding the time to run can be a challenge. There are many other reasons, but most of them really fall into a single category: Motivation. While there may be days when we are feeling great and ready to go for a run, more often it seems, we are tired or the weather is not optimal. But, if you are motivated enough, nothing can stop you from getting in your run. As a matter of fact, even the time issue may come down to lack of motivation. We almost always find time to do the things that are most important to us. While running may rightfully not be at the top of the list, it should be higher than watching television.

Motivation is defined as the process that initiates, guides, and maintains goal- oriented behaviors. It's what causes us to act, whether it is eating to reduce hunger or running to gain better fitness. It involves the biological, emotional, social, and cognitive forces that activate behavior. In everyday usage, the term motivation is frequently used to describe why a person does something. Simply having the desire to run is not always enough to initiate our action to actually do it. There are a lot of things we would like to do that we never do. Why? We don't have the motivation to initiate the action. We have to add personal benefit to the desire. Once we feel the need to do something, not just the desire, we will do it. Motivation provides the necessary impetus to convince us that we need to get out and run.

So, how do we get motivated? It doesn't fall out of the sky like rain. We have to find it. That means we have to intentionally seek motivation. Sure, there are occasions when a timely Facebook post will motivate us, but you can't rely on that to happen before every run. Here is a list of ways you can intentionally seek motivation:

Set Goals

Setting goals is the first step toward reaching a destination. Set short-term goals. What will you do this week or the next four weeks? Set long-term goals. What do you want to accomplish in the next year?

Begin with a long-term goal, like running a 10K or half-marathon in the next year. Work back from there. How many miles will you have to be able to run per week to get there? Do you need to increase the number of days a week you run? You don't want to do too much too quickly, so you will need to do a little more each week. You'll also have to consider rest, food, and what race you will you enter, among other things. Taking time to think about where you want to go and plotting your course will eliminate questions later, because you have already made decisions. All that is left is execution!

Find a running buddy.

Find someone you can run with from time to time. Knowing you're going to meet someone for a run takes the decision of whether or not you're going to run out of the equation. The conversation along the way makes the run seem easier, and it passes by much more quickly.

Buy some new running gear.

It is easy to go for a run on a brand new pair of shoes! Of course, you can't use this one too often, but it's a good one to save for a time when other things aren't working.

Read a book.

There are many books about running. There are classic books that have been around for a while, as well as newer books like Ryan Halls *Run the Mile You're In* or our very own *Run for God Devotions* (3 Volumes). There are books that will help you with eating healthier, creating training plans, learning tips for better running or even funny books. Reading about it makes you want to go out and do it.

Watch a running movie.

There are many great running movies out there and in the Summer of 2019 the Kendrick Brothers once again did what they do best. They clearly point people to Christ through the camera lens. *Overcomer* is a powerful film about finding our identity in Christ and how running can help draw those parallels. Other great faith based running movies are *Run the Race* which was produced by Tim Tebow, *Remember the Goal*, and *The Perfect Race* which were both produced by Dave Christiano.

Run a race at odd distance for an instant PR.

Find a race with an odd distance, enter it and no matter how you finish, you have a new PR!

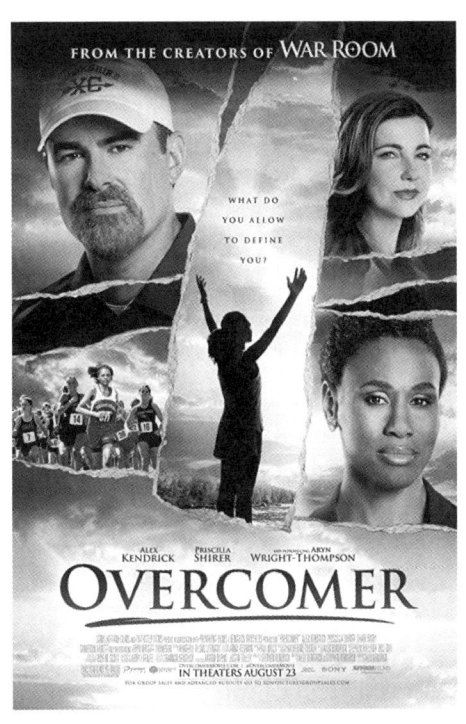

Find a Phrase.

Repeating running phrases can serve to keep you going when things get tough. Find a short phrase that keeps you focused when you need it. My calming phrase is "take what the road gives you." Some others: Turn and burn, One mile at a time, Almost Done, Feel the power. You can make up your own, just keep it short and to the point. Find the thing that gives you trouble, like hills, and design a repetitive phrase that will help with it, like "up, up and away."

Running Quotes

Find some good running quotes and post them in conspicuous locations. How about this one, "Remember, the feeling you get from a good run is far better that the feeling you get from sitting around wishing you were running." Sarah Condor. Or, "Pain is inevitable. Suffering is optional." Haruki Murakami. Or, this one from C.S. Lewis, "If one could run without getting tired I don't think one would often want to do anything else."

Leave your watch at home.

Go for a run without using your watch. Forget about pace, explore and notice things you never see because you're so attached to your watch and what it tells you. It's okay to have fun when you run!

Buy a GPS watch.

If you don't have a GPS watch, they add a new wrinkle to your runs. You can monitor your pace, your heart rate, and even the elevation, along with your time. Then you can hook your watch up to a computer, download the data, and analyze your runs. Perfect for a geek!

Find a great playlist.

If you like to listen to an MP3 player while you run, try finding a new, motivating playlist. This one can be very individualized. What songs make you want to get up and move?

Explore

Run down a road you have never before run. Go to a park you have never run. Try a new trail. Instead of running on the treadmill when visiting a city, go outside and enjoy the buildings and the scenery. Run in the morning and find a place to eat later.

Reward yourself.

Set a goal of running eighteen days next month and reward yourself with a pedicure, or a trip to your favorite restaurant.

Use your run time as extra prayer time.

Do you have a burden to pray for someone or something extensively? Of course, being quiet and still is our main time to pray, but talking to God while you run is just extra time with Him!

Run a race for your favorite charity.

Sign up for a race that benefits your favorite charity. It will help give you the will to prepare for it. Most races are run for a great cause.

Keep a log.

If you know you are going to have to write down a big fat zero in a logbook, it may motivate you to get that run in. Keeping a log also allows you to go back over what you have already done and marvel at what you have accomplished.

Take a break.

Take some time off. It may be just what you need to get re-energized.

Run at a different time of day.

Do you normally run in the afternoon? Try getting up early and going for a run in the morning. Do you usually run in the morning? How about going to a park after work.

Run in the rain.

Raining outside? Go for a run anyway! It'll make you feel like a kid. Don't forget to find a puddle to stomp through.

Run long.

What is your longest run? Plan to run longer.

Look in the mirror every day.

If you don't have a full-length mirror, get one. Look in it every day and either watch the improvement, or know that if you don't go for your run, it may be less appealing tomorrow.

Run from point to point.

Run from one place to another. I run to my grandson's football games. It's a great way to get in a long run and break up the monotony of running the same course all the time. Run to the next town and have your spouse come pick you up.

Make a massage appointment.

If you have never had a massage, it feels great. Tell yourself that you deserve it for putting in the miles. In addition, it will make your ensuing runs feel better too.

The decision has already been made.

Don't allow yourself the flexibility to decide not to run. Make up your mind before the day begins and follow through on your plans. The decision has already been made.

Don't expect every day to be better than the last.

Sometimes runners set themselves up for failure by thinking that they should feel better and running should be easier every day. Be prepared for bad days and just get through them. If you didn't have bad days, you wouldn't have anything to compare with the good days.

Focus on the competition.

Who are you trying to catch? Who are you trying to hold off? Focus on them. Do you think he is sitting on the couch when he should be running? Do you think she is cutting her workouts short? Friendly competition is great motivation.

Try a Tri.

Register for a short triathlon and train for it. You're not a swimmer, you say? Triathlons are full of people who were not swimmers at one time. Try it, you may like it.

Week 7 : Motivation and Jesus Wept

Run instead of doing the dishes.

Do you have a chore to do? Now, running sounds better, huh? Go out and run and do the dishes later.

Think about how much better you feel.

You know you feel better when you run. You sleep better. You have more energy. You're more alert. Why would you want to give that up? Focus on how much better you feel because you run.

Never take for granted the ability to run.

Remember what a privilege it is to run. There are many who cannot run, and even more who have never had the determination to get off the couch and run. You have that determination!

Don't compare yourself to others.

What's that you say? You're not very fast? So what! You are a runner. You run. It's what runners do, regardless of speed. A mile is a mile whether it is covered in seven minutes or fifteen minutes.

Be creative with your workouts.

Do something different. Bored with running repeats on the track? Run them on the road. You don't run any special workouts? Try running harder from one pole or sign to the next. Slow down for a bit and then do it again.

Visit a running store.

Local running stores are full of people who love to run. If the merchandise doesn't get you pumped up, the conversation will.

Take a running vacation.

Go on a vacation to a location where the running is great. Or, register for a race in a destination city. Enjoy your visit to the city before and after the race. Those larger races are always fun too!

Quote of the Week

"The man who wants to do something will find a way; a man who doesn't will find an excuse." Stephen Dolley, Jr.

Notes

Week 7 : Motivation and Jesus Wept

Workout Journal

Week 7

Workout #1
Start with a brisk 5-minute warm-up walk.
Jog 5 Minutes
Walk 3 Minutes
Jog 5 Minutes
Walk 3 Minutes
Jog 5 Minutes
5 minute cool-down walk.

Total Workout = 31 Minutes

Workout #2 and 3
Start with a brisk 5-minute warm-up walk.
Jog 8 Minutes
Walk 5 Minutes
Jog 8 Minutes
5 minute cool-down walk.

Total Workout = 31 Minutes

Be sure to download The 5K Challenge App which can be found in your app store.

Workout #1

Date _____ Distance _____ Time _____

Notes _____

_____

Weather _____

Workout #2

Date _____ Distance _____ Time _____

Notes _____

_____

Weather _____

Workout #3

Date _____ Distance _____ Time _____

Notes _____

_____

Weather _____

5-Minute Mile
Equals a 15-Minute Mile

Week 8

Take Personal Inventory

What are my goals for this week?
_____
_____
_____
_____

What are the things that I need to pray for this week?
_____
_____
_____
_____

What are the challenges that potentially lay ahead this week?
_____
_____
_____
_____

Reflect back on the past week and take inventory. What went right? What went wrong? What were some of the highlights? Be specific.

Week 8 : 5 Minute Mile and Concerto #55

Main Story Concerto #55 - The Music of God

My running has become an exercise for praising God, intercession, seeking direction, and listening for His promptings. This is my journal entry for October 13th 2013: It was a beautiful October afternoon with scenery you might see on a calendar of the fall months. A steady and, at times, a stiff breeze out of the west kept the temperature in a range of coolness that signals the warmth of summer is behind us and the colder temperatures of fall and winter are soon coming to Minnesota.

As I turned right onto the Main Street it did not take long for me to realize that this would not be a typical run as I had described above. There were no prayers of intercessions, promptings, new ideas, or insights that came into my spirit as I continued jogging on Main Street. I have to admit, at that point I was searching for direction from the Lord. I turned the corner by the bus garage and headed across both lanes of the road to get to the sidewalk (my usual routine) and headed up the hill toward the school. I still had no direction. I jogged past the bike path (the old railroad crossing) and then I did something I had never done before at the half-mile point. I crossed to the left side of the road as I jogged up the hill. I heard one word in my spirit - "Observe."

At that point, I realized that I do a lot of talking and not enough listening. Excitement about an idea or a change in my routine causes me to sometimes run ahead of the Lord, but I was quiet now and watched and listened. The sky was a bright blue with only a few thin, white cotton like clouds, which the wind soon scattered to reveal a clear blue sky. As I looked to my left, I saw the colors of leaves on the trees at edge of the field behind the cemetery, which ranged from dull, rust like reds and browns, to the bright yellows, oranges, reds, and a few green leaves who were fighting the changes of the season and were the last glimpse the summer greens. A group of small birds flew into a tree still clothed in fall colored leaves. They hid in the branches. One lone bird from the group sang a solo. If I could have seen where the birds sat, I imagined that they would look like notes on a musical staff, which was the tune for the little bird. The little bird's song faded, and another bird took up the song with his/her own tune, but I could not see the location of that bird either. This pattern of one hidden bird singing and then another bird picking up the song continued throughout the run.

I reached the top of the hill, by the school and the pine grove to my left contributed to nature's musical concert. The wind howled and whistled through the pines and became very loud. As I headed back down the hill jogging on the sidewalk, I noticed that a few trees on the right side of the road had lost their leaves at the top. The bare branches as they waved in the wind resembled arms lifted toward heaven praising God. Further down the hill there was a group of birch trees, which still had their yellow leaves. The leaves waved in the wind making a soft rustling sound and resembled many small finger cymbals.

I crossed the bridge as I continued jogging and I heard the sound of the river as it flowed under the bridge. The water made its way past the bends in the shoreline, gurgled its way past obstacles, and rippled the water as it flowed. Another bird picked up the tune of nature's music as I continued down the last part of the hill. Falling leaves danced in front of me and they looked like a group of ballerinas as they jumped, leaped, and a few of the leaves even pirouetted as the wind carried them and then they would lightly touch down. Then another set of leaves would continue the dance.

My feet picked up the rhythm of the music as I ran through a carpet-like patch of dry multicolored leaves. It was like a rhythmic tap dance. The dry leaves under my shoes providing the sound of the tapping. As I turned right at the corner onto Main Street, I realized that God had given me an awesome concert in His beautiful creation. I praised Him for all the things He had shown me with only one prompt - "Observe!"

I arrived back home and cooled off in the backyard. I closed my eyes to block out all distractions and to reflect on what the Lord had prompted me to observe. The wind had subsided and with my eyes still closed the warmth of the sun felt good physically and was also comforting to my spirit. One last bird sang from a tree somewhere in my backyard. It was not as melodic as the others, but it was louder than the others. In Psalm 100, it says, "Make a joyful noise to the Lord!" That bird was definitely making a joyful noise.

Here are a few things I learned from this run: 1. Each bird I heard was singing his unique song, and the other sounds, sights, and colors of nature all reflected the glory of God's creation. I want to praise and observe what God wants me to observe, so I can sing His song for my life, where I live. 2. I wonder how many things I may have missed from the Lord because of the busyness of my day, my routine, and my insistence on making my agenda the one I follow and then attaching the Lord's name to it (running ahead of the Lord). I want to work on His agenda each day (Listen). 3. I also realize the importance of not letting my time in God's Word, my prayers, and my daily walk with Him become merely a daily routine. My desire is to come to God's Word in prayer each day with an expectant mind, heart, and spirit to hear and "Observe," and let Him lead me into His adventure, which He plans for me each day. I checked the town thermometer after the run. It registered 55 degrees, thus the title: "Concerto #55!" According to the website: www.biblestudy.org "The number 5 symbolizes God's grace, goodness and favor towards humans. Five is the number of grace, and multiplied by itself, which is 25 is 'grace upon grace' (John 1:16)". God had definitely given me grace upon grace on this memorable run and gives His grace to us each day if we will listen and "Observe."

Dave Naslund - Onamia, MN

Get in the Word

Make a joyful shout to the Lord, all you lands! Serve the Lord with gladness; Come before His presence with singing. Know that the Lord, He is God; It is He who has made us, and not we ourselves; We are His people and the sheep of His pasture. Enter into His gates with thanksgiving, And into His courts with praise. Be thankful to Him, and bless His name. For the Lord is good; His mercy is everlasting, And His truth endures to all generations. Psalm 100

Trust in the Lord with all your heart, And lean not on your own understanding; In all your ways acknowledge Him, And He shall direct your paths. Proverbs 3:5 - 6

My son, if you receive my words, And treasure my commands within you, So that you incline your ear to wisdom, And apply your heart to understanding;

Yes, if you cry out for discernment, And lift up your voice for understanding, If you seek her as silver, And search for her as for hidden treasures; Then you will understand the fear of the Lord, And find the knowledge of God. For the Lord gives wisdom; From His mouth come knowledge and understanding; He stores up sound wisdom for the upright; He is a shield to those who walk uprightly; Proverbs 2:1 - 7

Something to Ponder

What part does praising the Lord play during your daily devotion and your daily walk?

Are there areas of your life that have become your agenda or routine and you have attached God's name to it?

What areas of your life or parts of your day is God prompting you to observe, listen, and be more perceptive?

When a 5-Minute Mile equals a 15-Minute Mile

Let me describe who I (Dean) am before covering a subject that has become increasingly important to me over the last few years. I have been running my entire life. I have been moderately successful and continue to compete at a fairly high level. At the time of this writing, I am nearly fifty years old and recently ran a 16:39 5K and a 35:00 10K on the grass. Those are pretty fast times, especially for an old guy.

While I don't like to brag about my accomplishments, it is important that you know who is writing this chapter, because there are misconceptions about being "fast" or "slow."

I've had running related discussions on every conceivable running topic with so many people, I've forgotten more than I remember (there's that age thing again). I have heard a disturbing trend in many of those conversations. More often than not, the conversation begins with, "Well, I'll never be as fast as you…" or "I'm not a real runner, like you, but…." What is it with the self-deprecating, qualifying statements? I want to say this as plainly as I can: YOU ARE A RUNNER. There is nothing to add, unless you want to say something like, "I am a proud runner," or "I am an avid runner." As long as it is something positive, you can add it.

It is okay to be slower than other people, but don't call yourself slow. We know that negative thinking is not good for us, so why do we accept it when we talk about running? You may never be a world-class athlete, but you are limiting yourself when you constantly try to convince yourself that you're slow. Negative thinking leads to performance that is less than ideal, whether running or your performance at work. When your performance is poor, it leads to more negative thinking, which leads to more poor performance. Eventually, you work yourself into a state where you don't want to continue. It can happen in dieting, running and anything else you tackle in life. Even worse, this pattern of thinking can lead to frustration, anger, or depression. Make up your mind to have confidence and leave the negative thinking behind. Instead of negativity, make positive thinking your new habit. It will benefit you in every area of life.

Running is running. Whether at the front of the pack or the back of the pack, there are similarities for every runner. Fast runners have doubts and fears too. While their fear may not be failing to finish a race, they are worried about time, pace and competition. The fear of failure for them is every bit as real as the fear you may have about just trying to finish without walking. All runners can relate to all other runners. Don't be intimidated by faster runners. Don't think you're not worthy to interact with them. The truth is that they feel the same way you do about a lot of things. When they run a PR, they are just as excited as you are when you do.

So, here is a secret about those people you may hold up as being "real runners:" Most of them are impressed by you. They know that being a runner is not always easy, and they respect the fact you're not sitting on the couch. Many of them even think you're awesome! For me, running comes easy, but I'm smart enough and see enough to know that it is not easy for everyone. If you're one of those in the majority who struggle to run, I am in awe of your determination! In addition, YOU are the reason us faster folks are often able to choose from so many races to run. Weekend races would be few and far between if race directors relied on only faster runners to show up. If you are a member of the turtle club, you're the reason for the event. Embrace your awesomeness!

There is always someone faster! There are a lot of people who are faster than me. I can workout with a college cross-country team and I would be the slowest guy there, but I didn't get slower, the people around me got faster. It's a matter of perspective. But, I'm not going to go home and sulk because I'm so much slower than those guys. I may even show up for the following week's workout to see if I can get a little closer to them. In addition, if you put that same team in the National Cross Country Championships, they wouldn't fare too well. Except for a handful of runners, there is always someone faster. Nearly everyone is a "slower" runner at times.

Why does it even matter if you're slow? There are very few benefits to being able to run faster that the slower runner doesn't enjoy. Sure, I have a ton of medals, trophies and trinkets that I have won over the years, but what good are they doing me? The majority of them are either collecting dust or in a box in the attic. I have a little name recognition locally. That's it. All the other benefits of running are shared by all of us. Being faster doesn't necessarily make me more fit or healthier, and it surely doesn't make me better looking! You retain all the important benefits of running that I do, and you're more likely to enjoy it because you're not so worried about shaving three seconds off your next 5K.

There are so many people who are unhealthy because they don't get enough exercise. You're not one of them. You are sacrificing your time and comfort to make a better life for yourself. You're already better than 80% of society if you do no more than that. There are so many benefits to being a runner that we all enjoy. You can climb stairs more easily. You sleep more soundly. You're blood pressure and cholesterol count is lower. You're more alert. You're just more fun!

I have had discussions with people that go something like this: She says, "I looked in the results from last weekend's race and realized I was 14th out of 18 in my age group. That's terrible!" And this is my response: "No you weren't." Followed by, "What? Yes I was. I just looked at it." And, finally, "But you were ahead of thousands who never had the guts to come out and start the race. You beat every one of them!" Always find the positive in all you do.

Running too fast leads to injury anyway. People who try to run fast all the time spend a lot of time on sidelines or hobble when they run. Be satisfied with being injury free. You can throw in some faster running to improve your times, but let the body heal. The faster runners are always right on the edge of pushing themselves too hard. Enjoy the company of running with others by running slow enough to have a conversation. You will still get the benefits of running without running so hard. Hammer less, enjoy more!

Use the energy you save by not running too hard to support other runners. There isn't a runner alive, fast or slow, who doesn't appreciate positive support. Be that person who everyone talks about when they say, "She always has a smile on her face."

Finally, remember this; you are an inspiration to someone. Let me say it again. YOU are an inspiration to someone. Whether you know it or not, there is someone sitting on a couch somewhere who is impressed with what you are doing. If you keep it up, you will inspire someone to get off that couch and begin running themselves. They don't care how fast you are. As a matter of fact, you are more of an inspiration than I am to a non-runner.

Quit worrying about being a fast runner. Focus your efforts on being a great mom, or being great at your job. Let running be fun. Whether you run a five-minute mile or a fifteen-minute mile, it is still 5,280 feet.

The Bible tells us in *Galatians 3:28*, "*There is neither Jew nor Greek, there is neither slave nor free, there is neither male nor female; for you are all one in Christ Jesus.*" We're all the same in His eyes. No one is better than another. The Bible also tells us in *Matthew 20:16*, "*So the last will be first, and the first last. For many are called, but few chosen.*" Hmmm, maybe there's a good reason to run slower! Seriously, some runners place such an importance on running that it becomes an idol to them. Whether you are fast or slow, make sure that running is a supplement to who you are and not the definition of who you are.

Quote of the Week

"Nothing can stop a man with the right mental attitude from achieving his goal; nothing can help a man with the wrong mental attitude." Thomas Jefferson

Notes

Workout Journal

Week 8

Workout #1, 2, and 3

Start with a brisk 5-minute warm-up walk.
Jog 20 Minutes
5 minute cool-down walk.

Total Workout = 30 Minutes

Be sure to download The 5K Challenge App which can be found in your app store.

Workout #1

Date _____Distance _____Time _____

Notes _____

_____

Weather _____

Workout #2

Date _____Distance _____Time _____

Notes _____

_____

Weather _____

Workout #3

Date _____Distance _____Time _____

Notes _____

_____

Weather _____

What is Run for God?
Are you ready?

Week 9

Take Personal Inventory

What are my goals for this week?
_____
_____
_____
_____

What are the things that I need to pray for this week?
_____
_____
_____
_____

What are the challenges that potentially lay ahead this week?
_____
_____
_____
_____

Reflect back on the past week and take inventory. What went right? What went wrong? What were some of the highlights? Be specific.

Week 9 : What is Run for God?

My Testimony

Week 9 : What is Run for God?

Main Story : Running Through the Dark

I just love running in the morning, it helps me wake up and gives me a chance to ponder life with God. The only drawback, especially in the fall, is that it's often dark at running time. This can be problematic for me for obvious reasons, but I still go out. Eventually the sun rises and I get some much-appreciated light to guide me. In fact, it is the very thought of "it's dark now but soon there will be light" that keeps me going.

It is very similar to how I started in my running journey in the first place. I had been married for 21 years with 3 kids and, out of nowhere, my wife decided to leave me and the kids and start a new life with someone she met online. I guess if I had looked close enough I might have seen it coming, but I didn't. At the time, I had been walking to try to improve my health and lower the risks associated with my type 2 diabetes.

On the very day I began running I had a particularly bad day. In fact, I was at a true low spot in my life. I was upset at her for putting me in a tough position, upset at myself for not seeing it coming and frankly, upset at God for allowing my kids and I to go through it. I was so angry I just took off for a run. I am not sure why to this day. Maybe it was out of anger in my circumstances, or maybe I just thought I would try to run from it, but either way, I ran. I found out I felt better after I finally stopped running that day. I called a friend of mine who I knew was a runner and told him what I did. My friend, Jim, then invited me to run with him. We would run, and when I felt the dark emotion of loss hit me, I would run harder until I ran it out. Sometimes I would even find myself crying while I was running.

Ultimately, I ran out of that "darkness" and felt the light that comes with peace. Jim and I kept it up for about a year, all the way through my eventual divorce. I would joke that our running was much better than the cost of therapy, and more effective in my estimation. Later, I remarried a wonderful woman named Theresa who had two kids of her own. Now we are working with blended families in our church. After a little hiatus from running, I have been back for about a year now. I ran my first half marathon and numerous 5ks. The best part of being back in running shoes is that while I am running I get to talk to the Creator of the universe about all of my problems and everything that stresses me and I can feel how much he cares for me. My most recent running goal is to complete my first full marathon. In addition, my friend Jim Sandefer and I have started a Run for God class in Akron, Ohio, with the goal of helping others run out of the dark and into the light.

Terry Price - Uniontown, OH

Get in the Word

For I know the thoughts that I think toward you, says the Lord, thoughts of peace and not of evil, to give you a future and a hope. Jeremiah 29:11

The sun shall no longer be your light by day, Nor for brightness shall the moon give light to you; But the Lord will be to you an everlasting light, And your God your glory. Isaiah 60:19

But if we walk in the light as He is in the light, we have fellowship with one another, and the blood of Jesus Christ His Son cleanses us from all sin. 1 John 1:7.

Something to Ponder

What circumstances are causing a darkness in your life right now?

_____

What ways whether it be running or other things can help you cope?

_____

Are you ready to trust God with those burdens today?

_____

Education : What is Run for God? Are you Ready?

A few years back, I (Mitchell) was in Richmond, VA for the Youth and Junior Elite draft legal triathlon. Some of our young athletes were competing, and it was an all around great trip. Something happened this weekend that happens quite often to our Run for God family. A gentleman came out of his way to comment on our shirts, more specifically, the suits our triathlon kids wear. He said that his son had recently come to know the Lord as his personal Lord and Savior, and when he saw one of our athletes on the course wearing his Run for God gear, it inspired him. That same day the remainder of the kids on our triathlon team were competing at another venue in another state. While getting a race summary from that venue, I heard the same thing; stories of how people had commented on the Run for God tent and the shirts. While making the eight-hour ride home, I pulled up my Facebook and began reading how Ben Reed, an instructor in Westerville, OH, had volunteered his class to work the packet pick-up at a local race. 14,500 runners were present. Guess what? They were all wearing their Run for God shirts, and to hear the impact they had on those runners was inspiring!

Yes, I am wearing a Run for God shirt 95% of the time, and I get many comments from many people. The vast majority of comments are great, inspiring, and are the type of comments that let you know the Lord has reached down and touched someone's day, even if it's just a small touch. Others are witty and even rude at times, like the guy that asked me, "What's God running for? President?" I'm convinced that in some way, even those people are touched with conviction.

So, can a t-shirt make a difference? I say yes, but I say that with a strong word of caution. People today seem more aware than ever of how others handle and portray themselves. A Run for God shirt, or any spiritual shirt for that matter, on the shoulders of someone who is out in the world living for Christ and reflecting Jesus can be a very powerful thing.

It says a lot about who you are and whom you follow. It lets others know what you stand for without you ever having to open your mouth. But, and here is the word of caution, you must be walking with Christ and reflecting His light for that shirt to have ANY power. I have a friend that had a quote printed on the back of his Run for God shirt. The quote is simply "Preach the Gospel, and if necessary, use words." That statement is so true! We can make all the statements we want about how we live for God, and even have a closet full of spiritual shirts, but if our actions do not backup what we are representing then we are only hurting the cause, and our words have no validity.

The above story was one that I wrote in our blog back in May of 2014. To this day, this type of story takes place almost on a weekly basis. The comments never get old, and I continue to be amazed at the impact that a Run for God T-Shirt makes. The reason that I included this story is because I feel that I stopped short of what needed to be said.

Yes, getting comments on a Run for God shirt is a great thing. It let's you know people are noticing and that's good. But what about those times that people "ask" about your shirt instead of just "commenting" on it? Or those times that you sense the Lord has put this person in your path for a reason? This is the time that the second part of the quote that I mentioned above comes into play, the part that says, "...and if necessary, use words." When someone asks you a question, it demands an answer, which requires you to use words.

So What Now?

Let's assume someone walks up to you and says, **"Hey, I like your Run for God shirt, tell me more about it."** At this point you're at a crossroads. Many times when people ask me this question I simply tell them that "Run for God is a 12-week Bible Study that parallels faith and endurance and takes people who have never run before to their first 5K."

This is a great answer, and it tells people the answer to their question. But sometimes we may be sensing that the Lord is leading us to keep going, and we must learn to get past the question, "What is Run for God?" and on to the answer to "What God has done in my life?"

I believe there is no better lead-in to sharing the gospel with someone than to share what God has done in your life. Your testimony is a powerful thing. It's truth, it's personal, and it's yours. No one can take that away from you, and no one can dispute the content so long as you're sharing what God is directing you to share. This is also a great way to build a rapport with someone, and doing so will make that person more receptive when it's time to start talking about eternal matters. We've all heard the quote by Theodore Roosevelt that says, "No one cares how much you know, until they know how much you care."

Practice

It may sound silly to practice sharing your testimony, but it's not! The Bible is very clear in that we are to always be prepared to share the reason for our hope. "But in your hearts set apart Christ as Lord. Always be prepared to give an answer to everyone who asks you the reason for hope that you have. But do this with gentleness and respect." 1 Peter 3:15, NIV

Very few people are active in evangelism, but we can all be prepared to share "our" testimony. Over the next two weeks, I want you to write out your testimony and be prepared to share it with someone. Writing out your testimony gives you a good outline to ensure that you have covered all the important milestones that have brought you to where you are. Many people think that because it's their experience, they'll be able to remember everything when the time comes, and that's just not the case. Does this mean that when God prompts us to share our testimony that we'll pull out our notes and read word for word what we have written? Of course not, but we'll have a framework from which to pull when the time comes.

Sharing your testimony is not complicated. It doesn't have to take a long time, and it doesn't have to be daunting like many of us make it out to be. It can really be boiled down to three main questions.

What was your life like before you met Jesus?

When and under what circumstances did you experience salvation?

What is different now that Jesus is Lord and Savior of your life?

Paul's Testimony on the road to Damascus Acts 22:3-21

"I am indeed a Jew, born in Tarsus of Cilicia, but brought up in this city at the feet of Gamaliel, taught according to the strictness of our fathers' law, and was zealous toward God as you all are today. I persecuted this Way to the death, binding and delivering into prisons both men and women, as also the high priest bears me witness, and all the council of the elders, from whom I also received letters to the brethren, and went to Damascus to bring in chains even those who were there to Jerusalem to be punished.

"Now it happened, as I journeyed and came near Damascus at about noon, suddenly a great light from heaven shone around me. And I fell to the ground and heard a voice saying to me, 'Saul, Saul, why are you persecuting Me?' So I answered, 'Who are You, Lord?' And He said to me, 'I am Jesus of Nazareth, whom you are persecuting.'

"And those who were with me indeed saw the light and were afraid,[a] but they did not hear the voice of Him who spoke to me. So I said, 'What shall I do, Lord?' And the Lord said to me, 'Arise and go into Damascus, and there you will be told all things which are appointed for you to do.' And since I could not see for the glory of that light, being led by the hand of those who were with me, I came into Damascus.

"Then a certain Ananias, a devout man according to the law, having a good testimony with all the Jews who dwelt there, came to me; and he stood and said to me, 'Brother Saul, receive your sight.' And at that same hour I looked up at him.

Then he said, 'The God of our fathers has chosen you that you should know His will, and see the Just One, and hear the voice of His mouth. For you will be His witness to all men of what you have seen and heard. And now why are you waiting? Arise and be baptized, and wash away your sins, calling on the name of the Lord.'

"Now it happened, when I returned to Jerusalem and was praying in the temple, that I was in a trance and saw Him saying to me, 'Make haste and get out of Jerusalem quickly, for they will not receive your testimony concerning Me.' So I said, 'Lord, they know that in every synagogue I imprisoned and beat those who

believe on You. And when the blood of Your martyr Stephen was shed, I also was standing by consenting to his death,[b] and guarding the clothes of those who were killing him.' Then He said to me, 'Depart, for I will send you far from here to the Gentiles.'"

When writing out your testimony there are some things that you may want to keep in mind.

Stick to the Point - Don't get off on side stories and distractions. Stick to the three main points.

Be Specific - Give specific dates, feelings at those times, and personal insight into what you were thinking. This will give the person who you are talking with something to relate to.

Be Honest - Don't dramatize your testimony to make a better story! Your truthful life story and how you came to know Christ is all the Holy Spirit needs to convict the other person of their sin and compel them to give their life to Christ.

Just Talk Normal - Share your testimony in a conversational tone. Talk just as you would normally talk and stay away from the religious lingo. You are who you are; so don't try to be someone you're not!

Keep it Short - There are times when making your testimony into a sermon is OK, but this is not the time. Keep it short, keep it simple, and let the Spirit work. Don't Be Discouraged – Not everyone who hears the gospel will respond. Remember that you are planting a seed that may sprout later rather than sooner. We are simply called to share and let the Holy Spirit take it from there.

Ready, Set, Go

Like I said earlier, take the next two weeks and work on your testimony. Use the outline that we've just talked about or make your own. Go in the direction that the Lord is leading you. Start by praying that God will give you wisdom through this process and that he will give you the words to say.

Quote of the Week

"I haven't failed; I've found 10,000 ways that do not work." Ben Franklin

Notes:

Week 9 : What is Run for God?

Workout Journal

Week 9

Workout #1, 2, and 3

Start with a brisk 5-minute warm-up walk.
Jog 23 Minutes
5 minute cool-down walk.

Total Workout = 33 Minutes

Be sure to download The 5K Challenge App which can be found in your app store.

Workout #1

Date _____Distance _____Time _____

Notes _____

_____

Weather _____

Workout #2

Date _____Distance _____Time _____

Notes _____

_____

Weather _____

Workout #3

Date _____Distance _____Time _____

Notes _____

_____

Weather _____

Steps to Peace
with GOD.

Week 10

Take Personal Inventory

What are my goals for this week?

_____
_____
_____
_____

What are the things that I need to pray for this week?

_____
_____
_____
_____

What are the challenges that potentially lay ahead this week?

_____
_____
_____
_____

Reflect back on the past week and take inventory. What went right? What went wrong? What were some of the highlights? Be specific.

Week 10 : Moving Past the Question

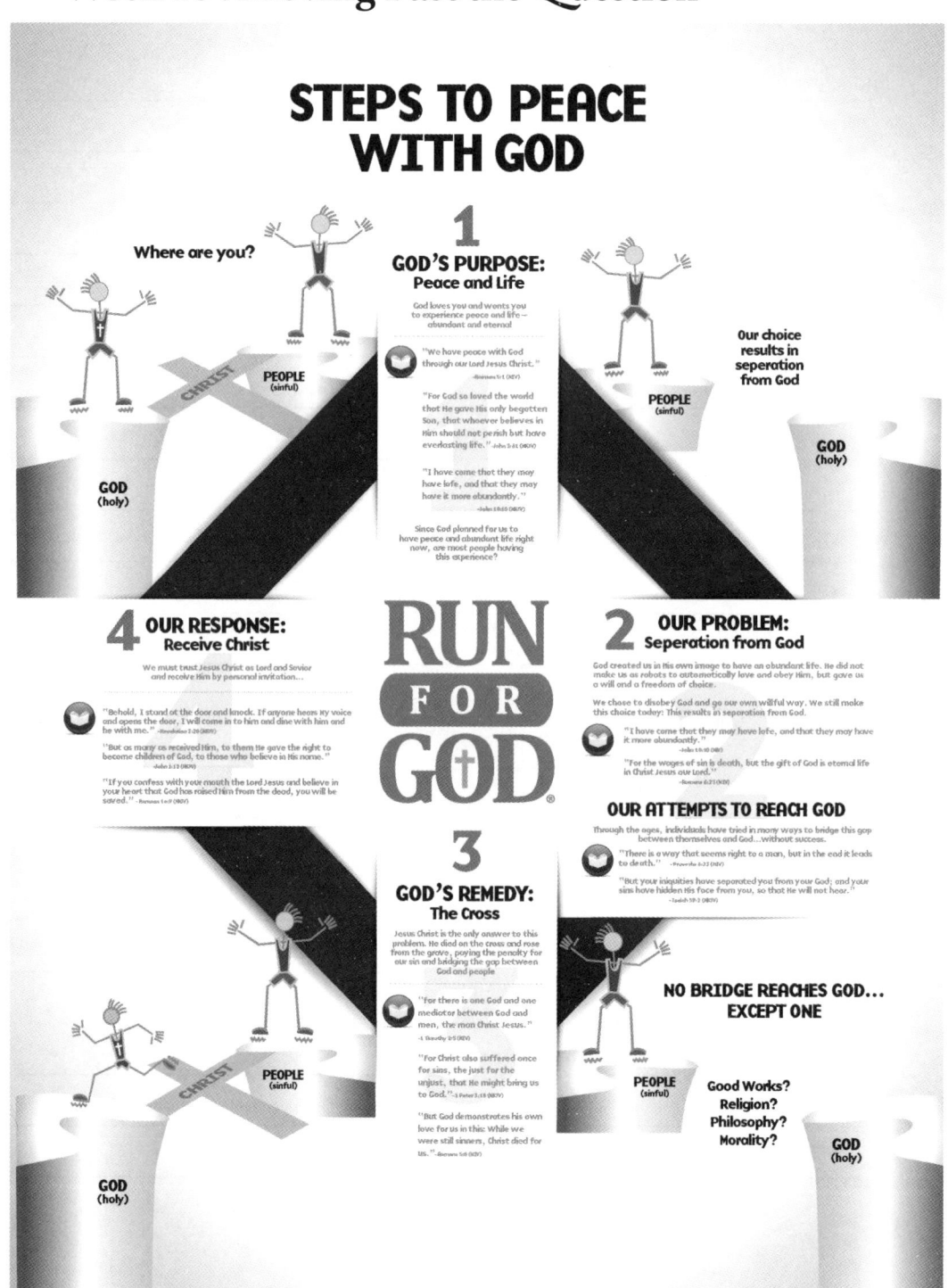

Week 10 : Moving Past the Question

Moving Past the Question, Steps to Peace with God

Run for God is a result of God moving me outside of my comfort zone. It's a result of God taking something that had become a barrier between Him and me and using it to draw me, as well as many others, closer to Him. But how?

Yes, it is my hope that people can see a difference in my life and in the life of anyone else that is part of this ministry, simply by the lives that we live. It's also my hope and prayer that the Run for God t-shirt would be used as a tool to point people to Christ simply by the statement on the front of it. Run for God. There is power in that statement, because there is power in the name of Jesus, but there are times that we must move past the shirt.

We've all heard the statement, and I even use it often. The statement is, "Preach the Gospel and if necessary, use words." We all interpret this quote to mean that we should live our lives in a way that would point people to Christ, which is what I shared in the previous paragraph. But the last part of that statement rightfully indicates that there are times when we must use words, and we must do so when the Holy Spirit prompts us.

It is at this point in our walk that many of us fall short. This is where the enemy will attack, and he'll do so aggressively. He'll throw doubt, insecurity, questions, and many other things your way once the Holy Spirit begins to prompt you to share the Gospel. We must continue through these tests, knowing that God has commissioned each of us to share the Gospel.

And Jesus came and spoke to them, saying, "All authority has been given to Me in heaven and on earth. Go therefore and make disciples of all the nations, baptizing them in the name of the Father and of the Son and of the Holy Spirit, teaching them to observe all things that I have commanded you; and lo, I am with you always, even to the end of the age." Amen. Matthew 28:18-20

The outline below is simply a tool. The Run for God T-Shirt has opened many doors to share the Gospel of Christ, but too many times we get hung up on the question, "What is Run for God?" when asked. It's time to move past the question and get to the heart of this ministry, which is pointing people to Jesus through the sport of running.

So then faith comes by hearing, and hearing by the word of God.
Romans 10:17

A Walk through the "Steps to Peace with God"

Family Introduction

Pair up with someone you either don't know or someone you don't know very well. Introduce yourself to each other and tell each other the name of one of your family members and who they are to you. It should go something like this.

My name is Mitchell. My family member is Holly, and she is my wife.

Go

Now, once you've done that, on the lines below write down your family member and who they are to you.

_____

_____

_____

Who is God? The Setup

Now, on the spaces below, write out your answer to this question.

In ten words or less, who is God?

_____

_____

_____

Go

Done? OK! Now, I am going to give you some of the more common answers, in no particular order.

1. He's the creator of the universe.
2. He's my Savior.
3. He's that guy they talk about in the Bible.
4. He's my King
5. He's the Father, Son, and Holy Spirit all in one.
6. He's my Heavenly Father
7. He's a Supreme Being
8. He's my Everything
9. God is love.
10. He's my Redeemer
11. He's Yahweh, Jehovah, and Adonai

Steps to Peace with God

So, you know who God is, you've heard of him, you may even know everything there is to know about Him, but the question is, "Do you have a Personal Relationship with Him?"

How did you answer those two questions?

I just told you that my answer to the first question was Holly, and she is my _____?

There is no other way that I would introduce her. You'd never hear me say, "This is Holly Hollis, she's the daughter of her mom and dad and graduated high school in 1996. No, I would only introduce Holly as being my wife, or my spouse, or my LOVE. I introduce her in a personal way because I have a personal relationship with her. The same goes for my children, my relatives, and my friends.

I'm sure it's the same with you.

It's not an answer that we even have to think about.

What about the answer to the second question? I gave you many of the top answers. You may have already picked up on what I'm about to say, but those answers fall into two different categories.

Relationships and Facts

Facts	Relationship
Creator of the Universe	My Savior
The Guy in the Bible	My King
Father, Son, Holy Spirit	My Heavenly Father
A Sepreme Being	My Everything
Love	My Redeemer

You see, all of the answers are correct, but one set defines a relationship while the other defines knowledge.

No, I'm not saying that if your answer was "Creator of the Universe," then you don't have a personal relationship with Jesus Christ. That's not what I'm saying at all, but it's a good place to start a discussion.

"Who is God to YOU?"
Mark Yoho, Fourth Watch Ministries

You see, many people in today's society think that knowing who God is and doing the things that we are "supposed to do" is the secret to having a personal relationship with Him. Or, they think if they have knowledge of God, that if they do good and not much bad, if they go to a large brick building each week called a church, or if they're just a really good person, then they have a relationship with God. I love the Georgia Bulldogs. You could call me a fan. I know quite a bit about that school, I know many of the players names, I usually know when and who they're playing, and I often even wear Georgia gear on game day. But I'm JUST a person who has knowledge of the Georgia Bulldogs; I don't have a personal relationship with anyone on that team!

In the same way, having knowledge of Jesus Christ doesn't mean that you have a personal relationship with Him.

So, we've established the fact that many of us know about God, but we've possibly cast some doubt on the question of whether we have a personal relationship with Him.

You may be wondering what is the purpose of all this.

What is God's Purpose?

God wants you to experience PEACE and LIFE – ABUNDANTLY and ETERNALLY – and He wants you to experience it RIGHT NOW!

That's what God wants, and that's what His word says!

Romans 5:1 says, "We have peace with God through our Lord Jesus Christ."

John 3:16 says "For God so loved the world the He gave His only begotten Son, that whoever believes in Him should not perish but have everlasting life."

John 10:10 says, "I have come that they may have life, and that they may have it more abundantly."

This is what the Word of God says! This isn't something that I, or your pastor, or even Billy Graham made up. It's not something that I Googled or looked up on Facebook. This comes directly out of the Number One Best Selling Book Of All Time, and it was authored and inspired by the Creator of the universe. BELIEVE IT!

So what's Our Problem?

Our problem is our Separation from God!

God created us in His own image to have abundant life. But He didn't make us robots to automatically do everything that He wants us to do. He gave us a will and a freedom of choice, and that choice often results in us doing things that don't please God. This is known as SIN, and ever since the beginning of time, we, as HUMANS, have sinned.

Some don't recognize it as sin. Some call sin bad things, or things that are wrong, or things that just aren't right. No matter what the world may call sin, IT IS SIN. You can mask it all you want, you can say it's your right, you can say everyone else is doing it, that it's not illegal, or it's just one time, or that you were BORN THAT WAY.

Born that way?

Therefore, just as through one man sin entered the world, and death through sin, and thus death spread to all men, because all sinned. Romans 5:12

You're right! You were born that way, and so was I, I was born a SINNER! That may be how we were born, but that's not what we were created for, and that's why no matter what I might say, no matter what image I try to portray, or how I might justify it, I WILL NEVER BE COMFORTABLE OR HAVE TRUE PEACE LIVING IN MY SIN, and neither will you!

Sin is what separates us from God.

Romans 3:23 says, "For ALL have sinned and fall short of the glory of God"

We have ALL sinned!

Romans 6:23 says, "For the wages of sin is death, but the gift of God is eternal life in Christ Jesus our Lord.

This is why we CAN NOT accept neither our own sin nor ANYBODY else's! You hear people say, "Well you just need to accept it." NO I DON'T!!! The stakes are too high!

Week 10 : Moving Past the Question

What are some of Our Attempts to Reach God?

Ever since the beginning of time, people have tried to bridge the gap between themselves and God WITH NO SUCCESS! We've tried...

Good Works – Maybe if I do enough good, I'll get into heaven?

Morality – I'm just a really good person, surely I'm going to heaven.

Religion – I'm at church every time the doors are open, I MUST be going to heaven!

Philosophy – I know everything there is to know about God, so I WILL be joining Him.

Notice how people get more confident the smarter they THINK they are.

NEWS FLASH! Really good people, who do a lot of good, who are always at church, and have a lot of head knowledge about who God is, WILL SPEND ETERNITY IN HELL without a RELATIONSHIP with Jesus Christ!

Proverbs 14:12 says, "There is a way that seems right to a man, but in the end it leads to death."

Good works, religion, philosophy, and morality seem like the right path? But they're not!

Isaiah 59:2 says, "But your iniquities (or sin) have separated you from your God; and your sins have hidden His face from you, so that He will not hear."

SIN SEPARATES US FROM GOD! And no bridge reaches God except ONE. So what is that bridge?

What is God's Remedy? God's remedy is the Cross.

God sent His Son Jesus Christ to come and live on this earth for 33 years. He was born in a manger to a virgin; He was often ridiculed and chastised for what He was teaching. He faced the very same temptations that we do. He had the choice, and He could have sinned, but He didn't. He spoke truth His entire life and ultimately died a horrific death by being nailed to a cross and left there. But a miraculous thing happened three days later: He arose because He was God!

This was God's plan.

1 John 2:2 says, "He (meaning Jesus) Himself is the propitiation (payment) for our sins, and not for ours only, but also for the entire world."

Jesus paid the price for our sins, and He did it on the cross with His blood.

Chris Tomlin sings a song that's straight out of 2 Corinthians 5:21. He says, "He became sin who knew no sin, that we might become His righteousness, He humbled Himself and carried the cross."

This was a game changer! We have the opportunity to become "Righteous" in God's eyes!

Righteousness is defined as "the quality of being morally right or justifiable."

YOU MUST BE RIGHTEOUS TO ENTER HEAVEN, and God gives us that opportunity through the blood of Jesus! WOW!

1 Timothy 2:5 says, "For there is one God and one mediator between God and men, the Man Christ Jesus."

Week 10 : Moving Past the Question

1 Peter 3:18 says, "For Christ suffered once for sins, the just for the unjust, that He might bring us to God."

Romans 5:8 says, "But God demonstrates His own love for us in this: While we were still sinners, Christ died for us."

There is only one way! It's not religion, it's not being a good person, and it's not having a lot of knowledge. We can become righteous in God's eyes, but we MUST do it by the way of the Cross!

God has provided us with THE ONLY WAY, but ONLY YOU can make that choice. You may be saying, WHAT CHOICE?

The Choice to Respond and Receive Christ

Respond to What?

Respond to Christ! For those of you who don't have a personal relationship with Christ, then with all probability He's knocking right now. The gift is right in front of you, the price has been paid, and all you have to do is accept it. Being a child of God is not complicated; you don't have to get your life in order first. All you have to do is trust Jesus as your Lord and Savior and receive Him by personal invitation right now!

Revelations 3:20 says, "Behold, I stand at the door and knock. If anyone hears My voice and opens the door, I will come in to him and dine with him, and he with Me."

John 1:12 says, "But as many as received Him, to them He gave the right to become children of God, to those who believe in His name."

Romans 10:9 says, "If you confess with your mouth the Lord Jesus and believe in your heart that God has raised Him from the dead, you will be saved."

Not may be saved, but WILL BE SAVED.

So where are you RIGHT NOW? Are you on the world's team? Or are you on God's team?

Is He knocking on the door of your heart right now? Are you feeling that uncomfortable feeling, like your heart is telling you what you need to do, but everything else is saying no way? That's a spiritual battle being fought right now between your sinful flesh and a Holy God.

Is there any reason why you can't be on God's team today? Why you can't receive Jesus Christ as your personal Lord and Savior RIGHT NOW?

For those of you who are fighting that battle right now, I hope you're asking the question, "How do I receive Christ, resolve the conflict, and have Peace with God?"

You must admit that you are a sinner. You must learn to call sin what it is and confess it to Christ. Talk to Him and be specific. If you don't call sin what it is, and you just keep justifying it, then you'll never have peace. Take it to God!

Be willing to turn from your sin. This is also known as repentance. Repent means to "turn away" from your sin. Not just slack off, or cut back, but turn away! Does this mean that we'll never sin again. No way! But it'll be our desire not to sin and to use every option that God gives us to ensure that we don't. True repentance means we'll never be comfortable in our sin again.

Believe that Christ died on a cross and rose from the grave for you!
Remember, *1 John 2:2 says "He Himself is the propitiation for our sins, and not for ours only, but also for the entire world."* Christ died for YOU and ME!

Through prayer, invite Christ to come in and take control of your life through His spirit, and receive Him as Savior and Lord of your life.

Week 10 : Moving Past the Question

For those of you who are out there who know that God has been speaking directly to you, you know He's knocking and asking you to join His team. I'm going to ask you to bow your head and just talk to God. If you want to have a personal relationship with Christ, then I'll even walk you through a prayer to help you through this process. All you've got to do is pray this prayer with sincerity and your name will be added to Gods roster right away.

Pray this prayer.

Dear Lord Jesus, I know that I'm a sinner; I know that I fail You everyday, and I ask for Your forgiveness. I believe that You died on a cross for my sins, and rose from the dead. Lord, I turn from my sins and invite You to come into my heart and be Lord of my life. I want to trust and follow You as my Lord and Savior. In Jesus Name, Amen

If you just prayed that prayer, then Praise God!

The Bible says in Roman 10:13 "For whoever calls on the name of the Lord shall be saved."

If you sincerely asked Jesus Christ to come into your life, then you are a new creature.

The Bible tells us this in *2 Corinthians 5:17. It says, "Therefore, if anyone is in Christ, he is a new creation; old things have passed away; behold, all things have become new."*

The slate has been wiped clean!

Whether you just prayed that prayer or you prayed it 50 years ago, I challenge you to go out and share what we've just discussed. When people ask about your shirt, tell them about it, but quickly move on and find out whose team they're on.

Be Bold and Be Confident in knowing that this is what God has called us ALL to do.

Notes

Week 10 : Moving Past the Question

Workout Journal

Week 10

Workout #1, 2, and 3

Start with a brisk 5-minute warm-up walk.
Jog 27 Minutes
5 minute cool-down walk.

Total Workout = 37 Minutes

Be sure to download The 5K Challenge App which can be found in your app store.

Workout #1

Date _____ Distance _____ Time _____

Notes _____

_____

Weather _____

Workout #2

Date _____ Distance _____ Time _____

Notes _____

_____

Weather _____

Workout #3

Date _____ Distance _____ Time _____

Notes _____

_____

Weather _____

Lifestyle
vs. 12-Weeks

Week 11

Take Personal Inventory

What are my goals for this week?

_____
_____
_____
_____

What are the things that I need to pray for this week?

_____
_____
_____
_____

What are the challenges that potentially lay ahead this week?

_____
_____
_____
_____

Reflect back on the past week and take inventory. What went right? What went wrong? What were some of the highlights? Be specific.

Week 11 : Running with God and Lifestyle

Main Story : Running with God

I saw God today! I saw him in the dark clouds that parted just enough to let the rays of sun shine through. I saw him in the vibrant colors that are more vivid just before a major storm. I saw him in the reflections of the puddles I ran through. I saw God through the hawks that soared through the sky, riding off the current of the wind. I saw the Almighty in the various purple, yellow, pink, white, and blue flowers that sprouted up through gravel, grass, and forest.

I felt God today! I felt God in the drops of water that touched my skin and cooled the sweat and heat. I felt God today in the cool breeze that touched my arms and face, giving me goosebumps as I ran. It felt like I was being encouraged to go further. I felt God when I ran through the prairie grass and got tickled on the legs by the jumping grasshoppers. I felt God today in the rumble vibrations from the thunder.

I heard God today! I heard God when the wind swept between the leaves of the trees, on the grass from the prairie. Always reminding me that He's never far away. I heard God today when I almost gave up on the run. I saw the massive wall of storm clouds coming and got nervous. But, my thoughts were of the perfect quote. "Be not afraid, I go before you always... come follow me". I heard God today in the croaking of the frogs, the chirping of the crickets, the buzzing of the locusts, and the mooing of the cows in the field. I think I could even hear him laughing while watching the fawns playing in the field with their mother or the when the rabbits and squirrels were playing tag in front of me on the trail.

I talked to God today! I told him how I was feeling pretty down and frustrated with life as of late. I told him how I felt like I wasn't strong enough or good enough sometimes. I told him my fears for what may come in the future. I told him that I didn't know how to become the person he wants me to be. I told him that I felt tired, stressed, and fizzed out.

As I ran today, I know I could hear someone's footsteps along with mine from time to time. I would look around checking to make sure it wasn't in someone else's way but, no one was there. How do you explain that one? You don't try...you just know!

I ran with God today!

Laura Jarman – Joliet, IL

Get in the Word

Let us run with endurance the race God has set before us.
Hebrews 12:1

But those who wait on the Lord shall renew their strength; They shall mount up with wings like eagles, They shall run and not be weary, They shall walk and not faint. Isaiah 40:31

I can do all things through Christ who strengthens me.
Philippians 4:13

Something to Ponder

What are some storms that God has helped you run through?

_____

Where do you find Christ in your everyday life?

_____

What are some examples that cement your belief that Christ is with you always?

_____

Education : Lifestyle vs. 12-Weeks

Have you ever gone to a seminar or some other event that really seemed to inspire you, but the day after it was over, you did nothing to act on that inspiration? It's okay, we have all done it. Why? Here are a few reasons.

For starters, we're creatures of habit. Once we imprint behaviors on our mind, it takes intentional, focused effort to change. If we don't plan for that change and put markers in place to ensure we follow through on our intentions, we never experience the change for which we were hoping. Secondly, there are always time constraints. Our lives are crowded with things to do, and adding something else or putting forth the effort to change what we are doing complicates our lives. By nature, we don't like complications. We have to make time for change. Lastly, deep down, we are comfortable where we are in life, or at least we think we are. Going outside our comfort zone is not something that the majority of us embrace. In order to make permanent change, you have to accept you will be uncomfortable for a time to do it. But, understand the uncomfortable feeling is temporary and leads to better things, including a more secure feeling.

So, what do we do?

You have to WANT to change because it will take effort. Showing up for your Run for God class is much easier than continuing your efforts after the class is over. You will have to rely on your own motivation, and it's important to face that situation before it happens. If you do not put a plan in place before the end of this class, you will likely slip back into the person you were before you made your leap of faith three months ago.

Go back to the first class and look at the reason you wanted to become a runner. Has it changed? If not, is that motivation enough to keep you going? If your reason has changed, will that reason sustain you when the weather is worse, or you're going through a rough patch of life? Make provisions for the obstacles before you see them. If you have ever watched a 3,000-meter Steeplechase race on the track, you will notice that after one of the barriers the runners must hurdle, there is a water pit on the other side. Can you imagine what would happen if the runner had trained on the "easy" barriers and didn't know about the water jump until it was race time? The reaction would not be positive. What are your water jumps?

They will be coming, but you can prepare for them so that when they come, you will hurdle them as if you were ready for them, because you were!

More Motivation

It is a fact that the average person who makes running part of his or her lifestyle has a lower BMI than the average person who doesn't exercise. Obesity may be the most significant problem in America. Until recently, America was the most obese nation on earth, and we're still second behind Mexico. There are many health related problems that are either caused by obesity, or are exacerbated by obesity. The top ten leading causes of death in America are: Heart disease, Cancer, Chronic lower respiratory disease, Stroke, Accidents, Alzheimer's, Diabetes, Flu and pneumonia, Kidney disease, and Suicide. Notice how many of those things are more likely if you're obese. Also, notice that nearly every one of those causes can be affected positively with a regular exercise program. The health benefits from running are well documented.

With all the talk about healthcare in the news, we seem to be misguided. After all, most of that talk is really about "sick care," or what we are going to do once we are not well. If we are truly caring for our health, most of the time doing something about our health will be spent somewhere other than the doctor's office or hospital. We will spend more time exercising and eating better. Running gives us more time doing something about our health care and less time at the doctor's office worrying about sick care.

Some people will say that your heart only has so many beats in it until it fails. They say it trying to discourage running as a viable activity, but let's look at it more closely: If your heart rate is 72 before you begin running, that would mean that your heart beats 103,680 times per day. But, if you are a regular runner, your resting heart rate will decrease because you are strengthening your heart. Let's say you decrease your heart rate by 10%, an easily achievable goal. Your heart rate would be 65 now, but you would spend an hour a day with your heart rate elevated, say 140. When you calculate the total number of beats for the day, it comes to 102,000. You have saved 1,680 beats! While it's not true that your heart has a predetermined number of beats in it, it's nice to have a cogent response for those who believe it to be true.

If you are going to make a lifestyle choice to exercise more, running is as good as anything else. The cost to be a runner is much lower than most choices. There are no clubs to belong to and the cost of your equipment is very low. You can run almost anywhere, too. On vacation? No problem. Need to get in a short run on your lunch hour? That's doable. Running is flexible.

Why else?

There's the challenge of a hard run or race with the fire in your legs and ache in your lungs. Knowing that you are giving it all you have and have stretched yourself to the limit gives great satisfaction. The feeling of euphoria that accompanies a hard effort makes the trial worth it. When things don't go well, the introspection as you search for the weakness in your body or your mind makes you stronger than ever and more determined next time.

When running gets easy, and it does, the peace and serenity of being one with God's nature is an awesome experience. In the mornings, the stillness and quiet can overwhelm you, while the evening runs melt away the stress from the day. Running helps us to put things in perspective and keep them there.

In short, running can bring you closer to God. The one on one time with Him while running can be amazing. 1 Thessalonians 5:17 says, "Pray without ceasing." You can talk to God anytime, anywhere, even while you are feeling the firmness of the pavement beneath your feet. And that may be the best reason to make running a lifestyle instead of a twelve-week program.

So, which will it be; a new lifestyle or a twelve week program? Make running part of your new lifestyle after the Run for God class graduates. Your body will thank you for it.

Make a commitment by signing the statement below:

MY PERSONAL COMMITMENT

I want to make running for God a part of my life going forward. I know there will be barriers, and it will be tough to continue at times. I know I will miss scheduled runs due to circumstances beyond my control, but I am committed to getting back to running as soon as possible. Life happens, and I will not be perfect, but I will not give up. I acknowledge that giving up is part of Satan's plan and I will not let him win! I am only interested in God's plan for my life, and I know that He says:

"Or do you not know that your body is the temple of the Holy Spirit who is in you, whom you have from God, and you are not your own? For you were bought at a price; therefore glorify God in your body and in your spirit, which are God's." 1 Corinthians 6:19-20

I am going to run the race to obtain the prize!

Name_____

Signature_____

Quote of the Week

"Do not pray for easy lives. Pray to be stronger." John F. Kennedy

Notes

_____

_____

_____

_____

_____

Workout Journal

Week 11

Workout #1, 2, and 3

Start with a brisk 5-minute warm-up walk.
Jog 30 Minutes
5 minute cool-down walk.

Total Workout = 40 Minutes

Be sure to download The 5K Challenge App which can be found in your app store.

Workout #1

Date _____ Distance _____ Time _____

Notes _____

_____

Weather _____

Workout #2

Date _____ Distance _____ Time _____

Notes _____

_____

Weather _____

Workout #3

Date _____ Distance _____ Time _____

Notes _____

_____

Weather _____

Race Day

Week 12

Take Personal Inventory

What are my goals for this week?
_____
_____
_____
_____

What are the things that I need to pray for this week?
_____
_____
_____
_____

What are the challenges that potentially lay ahead this week?
_____
_____
_____
_____

Reflect back on the past week and take inventory. What went right? What went wrong? What were some of the highlights? Be specific.

Week 12 : Silent Running with God and Race Day

Main Story : Silent Running with God

Today's fast paced society tries to avoid silence as it seems awkward or uncomfortable in a conversation. Most people need some kind of noise in order to sleep at night. After the attack of 9/11, I'll never forget the strange silence in the skies as planes were not allowed to fly. After my grandfather passed away, my grandma would always have the television on with a ball game because she was used to that noise in the house. Our technological world has become so noisy that we forget silence has value.

I'm learning that finding the truth in life requires us to stop, look and listen to our own lives. This truth can be so depressing and scary that so many of us try to avoid it. But I believe the true peace that only God can provide us is shown to us when we are silent.

Sports are full of noises and sounds that define them, but running has become my opportunity to embrace the silence and run with God. Silence isn't empty - it's full of answers. Running is a great opportunity to pray but also to listen. The most profound statements are often revealed in silence and the words LISTEN and SILENT are spelled with the same letters. We all know people who have an opinion on everything and are always willing to express it. Many times it is the people who are disciplined - who rarely give their opinion - that speak with meaning and importance. They have listened and thought before speaking.

I have stuck my foot in my mouth more than once and regretted saying or doing something out of anger or jealousy. The best thing I can do when angry, anxious, or disappointed is to take a quiet run and talk to God. This patience and silence when angry is a sign of maturity for which we all need to strive. I love running 5K's with other runners or training with friends that can push me and motivate me, but my most satisfying runs are on my own. Along with the physical benefits of running, this quiet time to focus on God has helped me grow in my faith. Some of my best runs are when I can relax to the point that I can hear nothing but my breathing and appreciate all the things God has provided for me. I'm always amazed how

Week 12 : Silent Running with God and Race Day

fast these runs seem to go when I'm able to quiet my mind and let my soul speak.

Today's world is full of challenges and adversity that can make it difficult to relax the body and mind. I once heard a quote that said, "Work hard in silence, let success be your noise." We need to find more silence in our life on Earth so we can make all the noise we want in Heaven when we finish the race with God!

John Hancock – Beloit, OH

Get in the Word

He makes me lie down in green pastures, he leads me beside quiet waters.
Psalm 23:2

And let the peace of God rule in your hearts, to which
also you were called in one body; and be thankful.
Colossians 3:15

These things I have spoken to you, that in Me you may have peace. In the world you will have tribulation; but be of good cheer, I have overcome the world.
John 16:33

Something to Ponder

What are the noises in your life that distract your Run with God?

_____

Why does silence seem uncomfortable for many of us?

_____

How can you create more silent time in your own life to focus on God?

_____

Education : Race Day

You've invested a lot of time and effort into your upcoming race. You want to be ready to perform to the best of your ability. All runners, from the first time racer to the elite athlete, get nervous before race day. Being nervous is okay, but managing your nerves is key to having the most enjoyable time and getting the most from your body on that day. Here are some things to keep in mind to keep you focused.

Before the race

Understand that you are going to be with many others who are looking for the same thing you are. Although this may be another participant's 100th race, it doesn't matter. They are not looking at you as if you are a foreigner invading their territory. Relax and know that you will not be out of place and that most of those veterans are happy to see you out there! Keep reminding yourself that you have done the training. You may feel some anxiety and that's okay, even normal. Don't think you need to change something because you feel nervous.

Another common fear is the fear of finishing last. Don't worry about being last because, in all likelihood, you won't be. Most 5Ks are community events serving a community need. There are usually a fairly large number of walkers who will simply walk from start to finish. Even if you have to walk some of the course, you will probably not finish last. And besides, if you did finish last, so what? Once again, you will not find a bunch of seasoned runners at the finish line just waiting to see who finishes last so they can ridicule them. More likely, you will find them cheering you on!

If possible, take some time to cover the route before race day. You will feel much more comfortable if you know where you are going on race day. People are often worried about missing a turn and getting lost. While this is highly improbable because there will be other runners around you and there will be volunteers on the course telling you where to turn, it will help assuage the fear of going the wrong way and getting lost. It also lets you know if there are hills on the course and where they are so that you are mentally prepared for them when they are staring you in the face!

It may sound crazy, but take some time to close your eyes and visualize your race day. Think about everything from getting up in the morning, getting your gear ready, getting to the race site, to the race itself. Picture yourself performing exactly to your goals. By doing this, you accomplish two things: 1) You may think about things you will need for the race that you had not already thought about, and 2) You will be more calm on race day because you have already run the race in your mind.

Continue to eat what has worked for you in the past. As you get closer to race day, avoid eating anything that could upset your stomach. Someone may tell you to load up on carbohydrates before the race, but don't. Again, eat the food your body likes. Carbo-loading, as it is called, is strictly for long races that are going to take over two hours.

Don't try anything new in the days before a race. This is not the time to start wearing a new pair of shoes or new gear. Stick to what you know works and feels good to you. Don't buy a new outfit to wear for the first time on race day. If it doesn't fit properly and causes chafing, you want to find out before race day. You don't want to take a chance on letting anything interfere with having the best experience possible!

Get off your feet as much as possible in the days leading up to the race. Don't go out and mow the lawn or start that new painting project the day before the big day.

Get everything you will need ready the night before the race. What is the weather going to be on race day? Make sure you have proper clothing and take extra. Will you need gloves or a hat? Is the temperature going to change significantly on race morning? Do you have something comfortable to wear after the race? A dry t-shirt feels great after the race! In some cases, you will be able to pick up your race packet the day before the race.

If you get your hands on your race bib before the race, go ahead and pin it onto the shirt you plan to wear in the race. Make sure you write your name and emergency contact information on your bib, just in case. Get it all together and ready to go so that you only have to pick up your bag as you head out the door. It will eliminate the stress that comes from realizing you can't find the shirt you want to wear in the race.

A couple of things you may want to pack are a trash bag and some tissues. The trash bag can be used for several things, including sitting on wet grass. And you don't want to be at a restroom only to find out that there is no paper. Be prepared.

Race Day

Once the big day arrives, don't eat anything heavy that could cause stomach issues. Avoid high fiber foods and fatty foods. If you normally eat a large breakfast, don't do it on race day. Keep it light.

If you didn't sleep well the night before the race, don't worry about it. More than likely it will not affect your performance. Good rest in the week prior to the race is much more important. Set your alarm on race morning to allow plenty of time. You can catch up on any lost sleep after the race.

You can avoid some stress by getting to the race location early. You will want to have time to pick up your race number and write your emergency contact information on it (if you haven't already done it), go to the restroom, and get warmed up. If you're running with a group, you may want to meet so that you take a before photo. Designate somewhere to meet so that you're not trying to round everyone up at the last minute. You should have plenty of time for everything you need if you arrive an hour before the start.

Running a race will sometimes change our stride just enough to cause chafing in areas where we never chafed before. It's not a bad idea to take precautions by purchasing an anti-chafing agent and putting some under your arms, on the inside of your thighs, around the jog bra area, and on your feet. You may not need it, but it's better to have it and not need it, than to need it and not have it!

A common race mistake is dressing too warmly for the race. You are going to warm up once you begin to run. Dress as if it were twenty degrees warmer than it is. If it is a very large race and you need to stay warm while walking to the start, this is a great place to use that trash bag. Cut a hole in the bottom and put it on upside down so that your head is sticking out the hole you created. You will be amazed by how warm this will be, particularly if it is windy. You can take it off just before the race begins.

Set a goal for the race, but have a backup goal in case conditions are poor or you just have a bad day. Having something to shoot for will keep you on task and motivated for the entire race. It doesn't matter what those goals are. You may want to try to run a particular time, or maybe just run the entire distance without stopping. Your secondary goal could be a different time, or to walk no more than a few minutes. They are your goals.

Get to the starting line early. Take care of everything, and leave time to tie shoelaces and adjust clothing at the start. It would be a travesty to have worked so hard to get to this moment and have it ruined because you were stressed out rushing to the start line. For your safety, try to make sure you line up in the proper place. If you line up at the front and your goal is to run 35 minutes, you may get trampled. But also keep in mind that there could be a large number of walkers. If so, you don't want to line up behind them and have to weave your way through them at the start.

Race day brings excitement and adrenaline. By race day, you should have a fairly good idea of what pace you want to run. Avoid getting caught up in the excitement by running too fast from the start. You know what pace you should run. Start at that pace, and if you want to pick up the pace later, you will still have enough left in the tank to do it.

Both before and after (and even during) the race, take time to thank the volunteers. They have given up their time to be there to support you. Without the volunteers, most races could not take place. All volunteers love to hear that what they are doing matters to someone. Be that someone!

Keep moving. If you take water at a water station, there will be people behind you as you take that cup. Grab yours and move forward and away from the area so that you are not an impediment to someone else. Do this at the finish, too. Don't just stop when you cross the line. Again, there are people behind you, and you don't want to get in their way. Keep walking and let your heart rate come back down slowly. Don't sit down as soon as you can. You will feel much better the next day if you keep moving and take time to stretch.

After the Race

Most races have food at the finish. Try to find something with a mix of protein and good carbohydrates to help you recover better in the few days following the race. Consume those calories within thirty minutes of your finish time. Sports recovery drinks, energy bars or fruits, like bananas are great for recovery. Just remember to avoid being a glutton. Yes, the food is there for you, but make sure there is enough for everyone.

Get warm if it is cold outside. Your core body temperature will fall quickly once you stop. Take a dry shirt out of your well-prepared race bag and replace your wet, sweaty one. You'll feel better and stay warmer!

If it is a large race and you are running with a group, make sure you have discussed where the group will meet after the race. You don't want to walk an extra couple of miles searching for your friends after you finish running!

Don't be surprised when you are sore the next day. You can get over the soreness more quickly by doing something active. Do something low impact, like swimming, cycling, using an elliptical machine, or even going for a walk. Keep it very easy. After a few days off from running, get back to it!

Paul compared our faith with a race in Hebrews 12:1-2: "Therefore we also, since we are surrounded by so great a cloud of witnesses, let us lay aside every weight, and the sin which so easily ensnares us, and let us run with endurance the race that is set before us, looking unto Jesus, the author and finisher of our faith, who for the joy that was set before Him endured the cross, despising the shame, and has sat down at the right hand of the throne of God."

God wants us to be prepared for our daily battles by remaining faithful to Him, and He wants us to understand that our lives are not one hundred meter races, they are marathons. We need to focus on all the little things it takes to enable us to live for Him, just like we have to prepare for the 5K

Week 12 : Silent Running with God and Race Day

race we are running. The difference is that there are eternal consequences for the most important race we will ever run.

Quote of the Week

Praise God and tell others about your goofy looking shirt! Mitchell Hollis

Final Thoughts

Workout Journal

Week 12

Workout #1 and #2

Start with a brisk 5-minute warm-up walk.
Jog 3 Miles
5 minute cool-down walk.

Workout #3

Walk for 20-minutes

Total Workout = 20 Minutes

Be sure to download The 5K Challenge App which can be found in your app store.

Workout #1

Date _____ Distance _____ Time _____

Notes _____

_____

Weather _____

Workout #2

Date _____ Distance _____ Time _____

Notes _____

_____

Weather _____

Workout #3

Date _____ Distance _____ Time _____

Notes _____

_____

Weather _____

Run for God
other resources...

Devotions
finding God in a runners space.

RUN FOR GOD
www.RUNFORGOD.com
RUN FOR GOD
RUN FOR GOD
RUN FOR GOD
OGIO
RUN FOR GOD

STEPS TO PEACE WITH GOD

Where are you?

PEOPLE (sinful)

GOD (holy)

Our choice results in seperation from God

PEOPLE (sinful)

GOD (holy)

1 GOD'S PURPOSE: Peace and Life

God loves you and wants you to experience peace and life— abundant and eternal

"We have peace with God through our Lord Jesus Christ."
—Romans 5:1 (NKJV)

"For God so loved the world that He gave His only begotten Son, that whoever believes in Him should not perish but have everlasting life." —John 3:16 (NKJV)

"I have come that they may have life, and that they may have it more abundantly."
—John 10:10 (NKJV)

Since God planned for us to have peace and abundant life right now, are most people having this experience?

4 OUR RESPONSE: Receive Christ

We must trust Jesus Christ as Lord and Savior and receive Him by personal invitation...

"Behold, I stand at the door and knock. If anyone hears My voice and opens the door, I will come in to him and dine with him and he with me." —Revelation 3:20 (NKJV)

"But as many as received Him, to them He gave the right to become children of God, to those who believe in His name." —John 1:12 (NKJV)

"If you confess with your mouth the Lord Jesus and believe in your heart that God has raised Him from the dead, you will be saved." —Romans 10:9 (NKJV)

RUN FOR GOD.

2 OUR PROBLEM: Seperation from God

God created us in His own image to have an abundant life. He did not make us as robots to automatically love and obey Him, but gave us a will and a freedom of choice.

We chose to disobey God and go our own willful way. We still make this choice today. This results in separation from God.

"I have come that they may have life, and that they may have it more abundantly."
—John 10:10 (NKJV)

"For the wages of sin is death, but the gift of God is eternal life in Christ Jesus our Lord."
—Romans 6:23 (NKJV)

OUR ATTEMPTS TO REACH GOD

Through the ages, individuals have tried in many ways to bridge this gap between themselves and God...without success.

"There is a way that seems right to a man, but in the end it leads to death." —Proverbs 6:23 (NIV)

"But your iniquities have separated you from your God; and your sins have hidden His face from you, so that He will not hear."
—Isaiah 59:2 (NKJV)

3 GOD'S REMEDY: The Cross

Jesus Christ is the only answer to this problem. He died on the cross and rose from the grave, paying the penalty for our sin and bridging the gap between God and people

"For there is one God and one mediator between God and men, the man Christ Jesus." —1 Timothy 2:5 (NKJV)

"For Christ also suffered once for sins, the just for the unjust, that He might bring us to God." —1 Peter 3:18 (NKJV)

"But God demonstrates his own love for us in this: While we were still sinners, Christ died for us." —Romans 5:8 (NIV)

PEOPLE (sinful)

GOD (holy)

NO BRIDGE REACHES GOD.. EXCEPT ONE

Good Works?
Religion?
Philosophy?
Morality?

PEOPLE (sinful)

GOD (holy)